PENGUIN POETS

D 20

BORDER BALLADS

Border Ballads

➤➤➤-➤➤➤-➤➤➤-➤➤➤-➤➤➤-➤➤➤-➤➤➤-➤➤➤-◄◄◄-◄◄◄-◄◄◄-◄◄◄-◄◄◄-◄◄◄-◄◄◄-◄◄◄

SELECTED AND

EDITED BY

William Beattie

PENGUIN BOOKS

HARMONDSWORTH · MIDDLESEX

First published 1952

TO

JEAN

Made and printed in Great Britain
for Penguin Books Ltd
by R. & R. Clark Ltd, Edinburgh

Contents

The numbers in brackets indicate the order in which the ballads appear in F. J. Child, *The English and Scottish Popular Ballads* (5 vol., 1882–98) and *English and Scottish Popular Ballads Edited from the Collection of F. J. Child by H. C. Sargent and G. L. Kittredge* (1904 and reprinted). This order is set out in a table on pp. 11–12.

The text is based on Sir Walter Scott, *Minstrelsy of the Scottish Border*, 5th edition (3 vol., 1821), unless another source is mentioned.

5

CONTENTS

CONTENTS

CONTENTS

CONTENTS

Table of Child Numbers and Titles

11

Introduction

NOT so very long ago anthologies of ballads for 'the common reader' were all too plentiful. That time is past and has been succeeded by one in which the study of ballads has become a highly developed science. Even the most modest book on the subject may run the risk of being assumed to be a work of original research. It therefore appears to me desirable to make clear at the outset that, beyond liking them (some more than others) as poetry, I have no particular qualification for dealing with Scottish ballads. The pages that follow contain nothing about their historical background or their folk-lore, and the nearest that I have come to providing any kind of instruction at all is to give English glosses for words that might puzzle those who are unacquainted with Lowland Scots. The selection includes what appear to me to be some of the best ballads associated with the South of Scotland. For texts I have leaned heavily on Sir Walter Scott's *Minstrelsy of the Scottish Border*, and my arrangement follows his, the ballads that he did not print in any form or that are altogether unrelated to those chosen by him being added at the end.

A previous volume in the present series was devoted to Scotland's greatest individual poet, Robert Burns. Now we are concerned with the other body of Scottish poetry that, at its best, has most generally given delight. Except *Chevy Chase*, which is entirely English, all the ballads printed here have been handed down in the South of Scotland among people who relied not on books or notes but only on memory. Beyond that we know very little about their origin and growth, except that, of course, historical events narrated precede composition. The great period of the ballads in Scotland is from the sixteenth to the eighteenth century. Whether any of them goes back further than the late Middle Ages, when they first appear in any quantity, and whether the ballad is, to start with, a degenerate form of the romance – discussions such as these are irrelevant in a book issued only because the ballads are worth reading for their own sake.

Who created

> It neither grew in syke nor ditch,
>   Nor yet in ony sheugh;
> But at the gates o' Paradise,
>   That birk grew fair eneugh.

or

> Oh, little did my mother think,
>   The day she cradled me,
> What lands I was to travel through,
>   What death I was to dee

are 'questions above antiquarianism', and the only point of contact that the ballads are known to have had with any one poet is when Scott, the foremost collector of them, or his successors such as Allingham retouched and rehandled some of them, much as Burns had done with Scottish songs. Even then we do not know for certain how much is traditional ballad and how much Scott.

The ballads of one country and those of another often show many points of resemblance. It is not merely that some motives and situations are found throughout Europe. Features such as simplicity and directness of style and the straight plunge into the story are the common property of balladry. But the recognition that this is so has never prevented anyone from preferring the ballads of his own country or seeing in them what he takes to be peculiar qualities. Spanish writers will swear that there are no ballads like those of Spain, and so with Russians, Germans, Greeks, and Scots; all of which is but another aspect of what Fletcher of Saltoun had in mind when he said that 'if

a man were permitted to make all the ballads, he need not care
who should make the laws of a nation'.* In what follows and in
particular in what I have to say about *Chevy Chase* it should
therefore be remembered that I happen to be a Scot and a
Borderer. There is another point that ought to be mentioned
in any discussion of differences between English and Scottish
ballads, and that is that the Scottish have come down to us much
more exclusively by popular tradition; their corruptions are the
easy, unconscious results of travel from ear to ear, whereas
into the English there has often crept another and more assert-
ive kind of corruption, that introduced by the printers of stall
copies.

To come, then, to *Chevy Chase*, 'the favourite ballad of the
common people of England',† included here as a natural
accompaniment to *The Battle of Otterbourne*, in which the
same events are narrated, it surely brings us face to face with
essential differences between English and Scottish ballads. It is
one of the few English ballads to have any poetic merit, and
even then what an unimaginative performance it is, except
for a few verses good enough to excite surprise that they should
be in that setting at all!

> The child may rue that is unborne
> The hunting of that day!

> Theyr bodyes, bathed in purple blood,
> They bore with them away,
> They kist them dead a thousand times
> Ere they were cladd in clay.

In the Scottish counterpart that enchanting, inconsequent
moment when Douglas turns from his anger with his little
page and breaks into

---

* *An Account of a Conversation* (1704) in *The Political Works* (1732),
p. 372.   † Addison, *The Spectator*, no. 70, 74: 1711.

But I hae dream'd a dreary dream,
    Beyond the Isle of Sky;
I saw a dead man win a fight,
    And I think that man was I,

the touches, slight but sure, such as

The Lindsays flew like fire about,

with which the story is kept moving in action and interest, and the tenderness of the climax, from the concealment of Douglas's body in the bracken-bush down to the surrender to Sir Hugh Montgomery, are all fine vivid things in themselves and they combine to form a harmonious whole. It is true that tenderness and variety, with truth to nature, are the very qualities that Addison saw in *Chevy Chase*, and one can understand how much the poem meant to him and his age in contrast to the tastes of those whom he called 'our little wits'. But seen against a wide background of poetic revivals and developments the English ballads are crude and wooden, whereas the Scottish, uncertain and commonplace though they can often be, yet rise out of that level into a poetic and dramatic intensity that remains their secret.

What a delicate balance often preserves Scottish ballads from the banal or the unintentionally comic may be considered in the corrupt versions of some of them still circulating among country people in America. Scott was once told by Mrs Hogg, the mother of the Ettrick Shepherd, 'There war never ane o' my sangs prentit till ye prentit them yoursel', an' ye hae spoilt them awthegither. They were made for singing an' no for reading; but ye hae broken the charm now, an' they'll never be sung mair.'* This prophecy has held, to the best of my knowledge, in the Lowlands of Scotland; but in America

* James Hogg, *The Domestic Manners . . . of Sir Walter Scott* (1834), p. 61.

Border ballads are still sung, and, as far as the words are concerned, that means that the process whereby their beauty is transformed not only by forgetfulness and the accidents of tradition but, more fully, by the changes of civilization itself, still goes on. Lord Randal becomes Johnny Reynolds, and the 'eels boiled in broo', with which his true love once poisoned him, are transmogrified into 'rattlesnake and eel broth'. In another version he bequeaths her his fine horse and his buggy. My concern, however, is not to deal with transplantations or what botanists call 'adventive flora', but only to suggest the sensitiveness and individuality of the original plant. Readers who are interested in its growth overseas are advised to go to the collections of Cecil Sharp and Dorothy Scarborough and others and to their fascinating accounts of their ballad-raids. From the point of view of the lover of Scottish ballads, these introductions, with their lively descriptions of what ballad-singing communities are like, may often be far more valuable than the collections of texts that they accompany.*

In Scotland the South does not enjoy a monopoly of the best ballads. The tradition continued longer in the North and may be studied in the collections of F. J. Child and Gavin Greig. One Aberdeenshire ballad, *The Laily Worm and the Machrel of the Sea*, is so fine that I wish I could discover for it some Southern link that would justify its inclusion in the present

---

* One of the most interesting things that emerges from these accounts is the sense of immediacy whereby events described in old ballads are sometimes conceived to be quite recent. In Virginia a man of ninety told Dorothy Scarborough that he had witnessed the Douglas tragedy: 'It happened away back yonder in Mutton Hollow. I was there myself. Somebody got killed over the girl. I was there soon after it happened. Another man was after the girl and one man shot him.' (*A Song Catcher in Southern Mountains*, 1937, p. 114.) Another matter of interest is that in modern times entirely new ballads have been created by cowboys, Negroes, lumberjacks, and others. The singing of ballads in America may be heard now from gramophone records and broadcast programmes.

collection. As it is, I cannot forbear to quote part of it here (in Lowland spelling, to spare the reader the pains of yet another dialect):

> 'I was but seven year auld
>   Whan my mither she did dee,
> My father married the ae warst woman

world
>   The wardle did ever see.

loathly serpent
> 'For she has made me the laily worm
>   That lays at the fit of the tree,
> And o' my sister Maisry
>   The machrel of the sea.

> 'An' every Saturday at noon
>   The machrel comes to me,
> An' she takes my layly head,
>   An' lays it on her knee,
> An' kaims it wi' a silver kaim,
>   An' washes it in the sea.

> 'Seven knights ha' I slain
>   Sin I lay at the fit of the tree;
> An ye war na my ain father,
>   The eight ane ye sud be.'

> 'Sing on your song, ye laily worm,
>   That ye sung to me;'
> 'I never sung that song
>   But what I wad sing to ye.'

*

> He sent for his lady
>   As fast as sen' could he:
> 'Whar is my son,
>   That ye sent fra me,
> And my daughter,
>   Lady Maisry?'

'Yer son is at our king's court,
  Sarving for meat an' fee,
And yer daughter is at our queen's court,
  A merry suit an' free.'

'Ye lee, ye ill woman,
  Sa loud as I hear ye lea,
For my son is the layelly worm
  That lays at the fit of the tree,
An' my daughter Maisry
  The machrell of the sea.'

She has taen a silver wan'
  An' gine him strokes three,
An' he started up the bravest knight
  Your eyes did ever see.

She has tane a small horn
  An' loud an' shill blew she,   shrill
An' a' the fish came her till but the proud
        machrell,
  An' she stood by the sea:
'Ye shaped me ance an unseemly shape,
  An' ye's never mare shape me.'   ye shall

He has sent to the wood
  For hathorn an' whun,
An' he has tane that gay lady,
  An' there he did her burne.

This ballad shows in a particularly direct and stark fashion
at least some of the characteristics of its kind — the abrupt
beginning and ending with the omission of all that is not rele-
vant to the situation, the economy in words especially in
epithets, and the tendency to let the story unfold itself as far as
possible in dialogue. Even in these few stanzas something is

heard of the variations that can be produced on the simplest ballad-metre of England and Scotland. Take any piece in this collection, and within it you will find similar modifications, but to listen to anything like the full range of metrical possibilities, it is necessary to compare, say, *The Sang of the Outlaw Murray*, *The Lochmaben Harper*, *Johnie of Cocklesmuir*, *Johnnie Faa*, and two distinguished by refrains, *The Twa Sisters* and *Edward*.

Those who have travelled north by Carter Bar will have recognized the bleak country of the raiding ballads with its wan waters and brown bents. Coming further into Scotland, they will have seen some kinder features, bonny burns and lily lees and even, despite the depredations of two wars, some semblance of that fair forest in which 'grows manie a semelie trie'. If they have got to know Borderers, the understatements and brevities of the ballads will no longer surprise them. Nor has there been a complete disappearance of the clannishness, 'gude conceit' of self and family, pithy sententiousness, inability to know when one is beaten, and contempt for authority unattended by worth that run through, say, *Johnie Armstrang*:

> To seik het water beneath cauld ice,
>   Surely it is a greit folie –
> I have asked grace at a graceless face,
>   But there is nane for my men and me!

What *has* been destroyed by the Industrial Revolution is the last trace of the imagination, the sense of the supernatural that gives to *Tam Lin*, *The Wife of Usher's Well*, *Clerk Saunders*, and *Thomas the Rhymer* a special place in balladry.

> Is there ony room at your head, Saunders?
>   Is there ony room at your feet?
> Or ony room at your side, Saunders,
>   Where fain, fain, I wad sleep?

The tragedy of this speech is not unparalleled, but its unearthly setting is, except in the Border ballads themselves.

If otherwise their treatment of tragedy is more or less common to Europe, their humour is Scots. This obviously holds for the purely comic *Get Up and Bar the Door*, which deals with the situation in a manner inconceivable in another country and in which the setting is local, even the weather:

> The wind sae cauld blew south and north,
> And blew into the floor.

But it is true also of the shrewd, sly strokes that come into serious ballads. The doomed noblemen in *Sir Patrick Spens* are no more exempt from the national sport of amused, almost malicious observation than death and funerals in more recent times:

> O laith, laith, were our gude Scots lords
> To weet their cork-heel'd shoon!
> But lang or a' the play was play'd,
> They wat their hats aboon.

This keen sense of incongruity, this watchful eye on pride before a fall, does not spare Marie Hamilton:

> When she gaed up the Cannogate,
> She laugh'd loud laughters three;
> But whan she cam down the Cannogate,
> The tear blinded her e'e.

> When she gaed up the Parliament stair,
> The heel cam aff her shee,
> And lang or she cam down again,
> She was condemn'd to dee.

When we come to *Johnnie Faa*, the absurd is so thoroughly mixed up with the sad that we hardly know where we are. Not

21

that the bewilderment takes away one whit of the 'glamourie' that is 'coost' over us. In this as in so many respects the art of the ballads is elusive, and, the harder analysis is pressed, the more there remains to say. It looks as though the last word will always be with the ballads.

We have seen Addison praising them for their truth to nature, as Dryden had done before him, but the eighteenth century is well advanced before the printing of ballads begins to influence the poetry of the time. Their tragic depths and supernatural magic, which fascinated Chatterton, took possession of the great writers of the Romantic Revival and helped to shape the work of Wordsworth, Coleridge, and, in one or two pieces, Keats. Here we have the most profound and genuine influence that the ballads have exerted on literature.* At the end of the nineteenth century, when *villanelles*, *rondeaux*, *ballades*, and other antique forms were all the rage, there was hardly a poet who did not also show a preoccupation with ballads. Rossetti, Swinburne, Morris, Wilde, Kipling, and A. E. Housman wrote what looked like ballads or in what they conceived to be the ballad manner, or at least confessed to admirers that they had been influenced by the ballads. Swinburne in particular was fluent in pastiche of this remarkable kind:

> O weary fa' the east wind,
>   And weary fa' the west;
> And gin I were under the wan waves wide
>   I wot weel wad I rest.

An academic critic of the period, W Macneile Dixon, in an admirable essay reprinted many years later in his *Apology for the Arts* (1944), drew a clear distinction between the poetry of

* The lighter influence of the English printed ballads is also worth considering. *John Gilpin*, elegant *divertissement* though it is, heads the list of works that owe something of their genesis to stall copies.

the traditional ballads and the highly personal poetry of the nineties. He was living in an age of literary individualists. Among the authors whom I have named, only Morris and Kipling had any real sense of poetic tradition. Kipling's sense fixed on matters of craftsmanship. Morris, for all his occasional absurdities in verse, showed in this as in so many arts an awareness of the past and the future and his own relation to them. The result was that each of these two writers in his own way could be at ease with the ballads, as many of their contemporaries could not, and knew when to leave them alone, and when to absorb them, so that from the contact would come something at once new and old, like *Shameful Death* or *Danny Deever*.

In our time there is no longer to the same extent as in the nineties this need to emphasize the distinction between the ballads and modern, personal poetry. The individual talent has become subordinated to tradition. The twentieth century is more aware of the past, more open to influences from abroad than the nineteenth, and there is now not the same risk as formerly of a poet's becoming obsessed by the ballads of his country to the exclusion of other inspirations. Edwin Muir in the older generation and Kathleen Raine in the younger sometimes strike me as poets to whom the ballads have meant a good deal. But both have taken the ballads in their stride. In Scotland the dominant influences come rather from the individual poets of the sixteenth and seventeenth centuries — Dunbar, Henryson, Douglas, and Lindsay. The ballads have settled down quietly as one among many influences from the past.

Unless the contrary is stated in the list of contents, the texts are based on Sir Walter Scott's *Minstrelsy of the Scottish Border*, '5th' (really 6th) edition (3 vol., 1821), the latest that I have been able to consult of those published during his lifetime. It has been checked with the first edition (1802–03) and also with the first published after his death (4 vol., 1833), under the editorship of his son-in-law, John Gibson Lockhart. It was part of Scott's practice to adapt and rewrite his material, but not always at those points where he has been suspected of doing so; and some of the strictures made on his editorial faithfulness by T. F. Henderson (in his edition of the *Minstrelsy*, 4 vol., 1902) and by the Harvard scholar F. J. Child (in his great collection of *The English and Scottish Popular Ballads*, 5 vol., 1882–98) have been examined by M. R. Dobie in an article entitled 'The Development of Scott's *Minstrelsy*: an attempt at a reconstruction' in *Edinburgh Bibliographical Society Transactions*, vol. ii (1946), pp. 65–87. There is an excellent one-volume 'Child' edited by Helen Child Sargent and G. L. Kittredge (1904 and reprinted); and another careful choice of texts, with interesting notes, is to be found in Frank Sidgwick's *Popular Ballads of the Olden Time* (4 vol., 1903–12). Of those who have believed that, 'granting a "turn" for such things', the editor's business is to build up from the traditional versions the best single form and even to improve that by re-handling, the most successful since Scott's day have been William Allingham (*The Ballad Book*, 1864) and Sir Arthur Quiller-Couch (*The Oxford Book of Ballads*, 1910). Lacking their 'turn', I have had to be content with reprinting from the older collectors such as Ramsay, Herd, Caw, Johnson, Scott himself, and Jamieson what appeared to me, from the point of view of the reader of poetry, to be the best available version.

For criticism and history, W. J. Entwistle's *European Balladry* (1939; 2nd impression corrected, 1950) and G. H. Gerould's *The Ballad of Tradition* (1932) should be read, and the writings of W. P. Ker, especially his essay 'On the history of the Ballads, 1100–1500' reprinted in *Form and*

Style in Poetry (1928), and those entitled 'Spanish and English Ballads' and 'On the Danish Ballads' reprinted in *Collected Essays* (2 vol., 1925). Edwin Muir's essay 'A Note on the Scottish Ballads' in *Latitudes* (1924) is written with creative insight.

Sir Alexander Gray's translations of European ballads into Scots verse are contained in his *Arrows* (1932) and *Sir Halewyn* (1949).

*

Since these paragraphs were written,* M. J. C. Hodgart has published his excellent volume, *The Ballads* (1950), which is a strikingly just work, though perhaps the 'great revisers' of the eighteenth century came nearer the average taste of their time and countryside than he allows. There are not quite fair implications in calling Hogg 'a sophisticated literary man' – largely, it would appear, on the strength of his 'brilliant *confessions of a justified sinner*', which happens to have appealed of late to some highly sophisticated readers but is unfortunately no more typical of his prose than *Kilmeny* is of his verse.

* A printed source that has come to light near the eleventh hour is an apparently unique copy of Allan Ramsay, *The Tea-Table Miscellany*, vol. ii (1726), belonging to Lord Haddington, who has kindly allowed me to print from it *Waly, waly, gin Love be bony*, with the article whose absence from the later versions quickens the pace at the wrong moment in the line:

    And fades away like *the* Morning Dew.

Common Words

a', all
aboon, abune, above
ae, one
aff, off
aft, oft
ain, own
alane, alone
an, and, if
ane, one
anes, once
auld, old
awa, away
awin, own
ay, aye, always

baith, both
bane, bone
bauld, bold
blaw, blow
bonie, bonnie, bony, pretty, fine
bra', fine
braid, broad
brak, broke
braw, fine
burn, stream

ca', call
ca', drive
cam, came
canna, cannot
cauld, cold
claes, clothes

dinna, do not

e'e, eye

fa', fall
faem, foam
fause, false
frae, from
fu', full

gae, gave
gae, go
gane, gone
gang, go
gar, cause to
gaun, going
gear, property, especially cattle
gie, give
gif, if
gin, if
goud, gowd, gold
gude, guid, good

ha', hall
had, hold
hae, have
hame, home
haud, hauld, hold
hie, high

ilk, ilka, each, every
intill, into, in
I'se, I shall

kaim, kame, comb

ken, know

kye, cows

laigh, low

lane, lone, alone

lang, long

lat, let

mae, *mair*, more

mane, moan

maun, must

meikle, much

mony, many

muckle, much

na, not

nae, no

nane, none

onie, *ony*, any

or, ere

ower, *owre*, over, too

rade, rode

rin, run

sae, so

sair, sore

sall, shall

sang, song

sic, *sicken*, such

sma', small

snaw, snow

stane, stone

syne, then, next

the tane, the one

tauld, told

twa, *twae*, two

wa', wall

wad, would

wae, woe

wald, would

wat, wetted

wat, wot

weel, well

weet, wet

wha, *whae*, who

winna, will not

Sir Patrick Spens

The King sits in Dunfermline town,
    Drinking the blude-red wine;
'O whare will I get a skeely skipper,   skilful
    To sail this new ship of mine!'

O up and spake an eldern knight,
    Sat at the King's right knee, —
'Sir Patrick Spens is the best sailor,
    That ever sail'd the sea.'

Our King has written a braid letter,   broad, i.e.
    And seal'd it with his hand,   on a broad
And sent it to Sir Patrick Spens,   sheet
    Was walking on the strand.

'To Noroway, to Noroway,
    To Noroway o'er the faem;
The King's daughter of Noroway,
    'Tis thou maun bring her hame.'   must

The first word that Sir Patrick read,
    Sae loud loud laughed he;
The neist word that Sir Patrick read,   next
    The tear blinded his e'e.

'O wha is this has done this deed,
    And tauld the King o' me,
To send us out, at this time of the year,
    To sail upon the sea?

'Be it wind, be it weet, be it hail, be it sleet,
    Our ship must sail the faem;
The King's daughter of Noroway,
    'Tis we must fetch her hame.'

They hoysed their sails on Monenday morn,
    Wi' a' the speed they may ;
They hae landed in Noroway,
    Upon a Wodensday.

They hadna been a week, a week,
    In Noroway, but twae,
When that the lords o' Noroway
    Began aloud to say, —

'Ye Scottishmen spend a' our King's goud,
    And a' our Queenis fee.'
'Ye lie, ye lie, ye liars loud!
    Fu' loud I hear ye lie.

'For I brought as much white monie,
    As gane my men and me,
And I brought a half-fou o' gude red goud,
    Out o'er the sea wi' me.

'Make ready, make ready, my merrymen a'!
    Our gude ship sails the morn.'
'Now, ever alake, my master dear,
    I fear a deadly storm!

suffice

-bushel

tomorrow

'I saw the new moon, late yestreen,
　Wi' the auld moon in her arm;
And, if we gang to sea, master,
　I fear we'll come to harm.'

They hadna sail'd a league, a league,
　A league but barely three,
When the lift grew dark, and the wind blew　　sky
　　　loud,
　And gurly grew the sea.　　　　　　　　　　growling

The ankers brak, and the topmasts lap,　　　sprang
　It was sic a deadly storm;
And the waves cam o'er the broken ship,
　Till a' her sides were torn.

'O where will I get a gude sailor,
　To take my helm in hand,
Till I get up to the tall top-mast,
　To see if I can spy land?'

'O here am I, a sailor gude,
　To take the helm in hand,
Till you go up to the tall top-mast;
　But I fear you'll ne'er spy land.'

He hadna gane a step, a step,
　A step but barely ane,
When a bout flew out of our goodly ship,　　bolt
　And the salt sea it came in.

'Gae, fetch a web o' the silken claith,
　Another o' the twine,　　　　　　　　　　canvas

31

bind

And wap them into our ship's side,
    And let na the sea come in.'

They fetched a web o' the silken claith,
    Another o' the twine,
And they wapped them round that gude ship's
      side,
    But still the sea came in.

loath

O laith, laith, were our gude Scots lords
    To weet their cork-heel'd shoon!
But lang or a' the play was play'd,
    They wat their hats aboon.

floated

And mony was the feather-bed,
    That flatter'd on the faem;
And mony was the gude lord's son,
    That never mair cam hame.

The ladyes wrang their fingers white,
    The maidens tore their hair,
A' for the sake of their true loves;
    For them they'll see nae mair.

O lang, lang, may the ladyes sit,
    Wi' their fans into their hand,
Before they see Sir Patrick Spens
    Come sailing to the strand!

combs

And lang, lang, may the maidens sit,
    Wi' their goud kaims in their hair,
A' waiting for their ain dear loves!
    For them they'll see nae mair.

32

Half owre, half owre to Aberdour,*
    'Tis fifty fathoms deep,
And there lies gude Sir Patrick Spens,
    Wi' the Scots lords at his feet.

* This reading, found in Percy and Herd, is given by Scott
in a note; that in his text is 'O forty miles off Aberdeen'.

The Battle of Otterbourne

1 August
moor-; dry

It fell about the Lammas tide,
    When the muir-men win their hay,
The doughty Earl of Douglas rode
    Into England, to catch a prey.

He chose the Gordons and the Græmes,
    With them the Lindesays, light and gay;
But the Jardines wald not with him ride,
    And they rue it to this day.

And he has burn'd the dales of Tyne,
    And part of Bambrough shire;
And three good towers on Roxburgh fells,
    He left them all on fire.

And he march'd up to Newcastle,
    And rode it round about;
'O wha's the lord of this castle,
    Or wha's the lady o't?'

But up spake proud Lord Percy, then,
    And O but he spake hie!

high

'I am the lord of this castle,
    My wife's the lady gay.'

'If thou'rt the lord of this castle,
    Sae weel it pleases me!
For, ere I cross the Border fells,
    The tane of us shall die.'

The one

34

He took a lang spear in his hand,
　　Shod with the metal free,
And for to meet the Douglas there,
　　He rode right furiouslie.

But O how pale his lady look'd,
　　Frae aff the castle wa',
When down before the Scottish spear,
　　She saw proud Percy fa'.

'Had we twa been upon the green,
　　And never an eye to see,
I wad hae had you, flesh and fell;　　　　hide
　　But your sword sall gae wi' me.'

'But gae ye up to Otterbourne,
　　And wait there dayis three;
And, if I come not ere three dayis end,
　　A fause knight ca' ye me.'

'The Otterbourne's a bonnie burn;
　　'Tis pleasant there to be;
But there is nought at Otterbourne,
　　To feed my men and me.

'The deer rins wild on hill and dale,
　　The birds fly wild from tree to tree;
But there is neither bread nor kale,　　　greens
　　To fend my men and me.　　　　　　support

'Yet I will stay at Otterbourne,
　　Where you shall welcome be;
And, if ye come not at three dayis end,
　　A fause lord I'll ca' thee.'

35

'Thither will I come,' proud Percy said,
　'By the might of Our Ladye!' –
await 'There will I bide thee,' said the Douglas,
　'My trowth I plight to thee.'

They lighted high on Otterbourne,
　Upon the bent sae brown;
They lighted high on Otterbourne,
tents 　And threw their pallions down.

And he that had a bonnie boy,
　Sent out his horse to grass;
And he that had not a bonnie boy,
　His ain servant he was.

But up then spake a little page,
　Before the peep of dawn –
'O waken ye, waken ye, my good lord,
　For Percy's hard at hand.'

'Ye lie, ye lie, ye liar loud!
　Sae loud I hear ye lie:
For Percy had not men yestreen
deal with 　To dight my men and me.

'But I hae dream'd a dreary dream,
　Beyond the Isle of Sky;
I saw a dead man win a fight,
　And I think that man was I.'

He belted on his good braid sword,
　And to the field he ran;
But he forgot the helmet good,
　That should have kept his brain.

When Percy wi' the Douglas met,
    I wat he was fu' fain!   *wot; eager*
They swakked their swords, till sair they swat, *clashed;*
    And the blood ran down like rain.   *sweated*

But Percy with his good broad sword,
    That could so sharply wound,
Has wounded Douglas on the brow,
    Till he fell to the ground.

Then he call'd on his little foot-page,
    And said – 'Run speedilie,
And fetch my ain dear sister's son,
    Sir Hugh Montgomery.'

'My nephew good,' the Douglas said,
    'What recks the death of ane!
Last night I dream'd a dreary dream,
    And I ken the day's thy ain.

'My wound is deep; I fain would sleep;
    Take thou the vanguard of the three,
And hide me by the braken bush,
    That grows on yonder lilye lee.

'O bury me by the braken bush,
    Beneath the blooming briar,
Let never living mortal ken,
    That ere a kindly Scot lies here.'   *native*

He lifted up that noble lord,
    Wi' the saut tear in his e'e;
He hid him in the braken bush,
    That his merrie men might not see.

The moon was clear, the day drew near,
  The spears in flinders flew,
But mony a gallant Englishman
  Ere day the Scotsmen slew.

The Gordons good, in English blood,
  They steep'd their hose and shoon;
The Lindsays flew like fire about,
  Till all the fray was done.

The Percy and Montgomery met,
  That either of other were fain;
They swapped swords, and they twa swat,
  And aye the blude ran down between.

'Yield thee, O yield thee, Percy!' he said,
  'Or else I vow I'll lay thee low!'
'Whom to shall I yield,' said Earl Percy,
  'Now that I see it must be so?'

low-born

'Thou shalt not yield to lord nor loun,
  Nor yet shalt thou yield to me;
But yield thee to the braken bush,
  That grows upon yon lilye lee!'

'I will not yield to a braken bush,
  Nor yet will I yield to a briar;
But I would yield to Earl Douglas,
  Or Sir Hugh the Montgomery, if he were here

As soon as he knew it was Montgomery,
  He stuck his sword's point in the gronde;
And the Montgomery was a courteous knight,
  And quickly took him by the honde.

This deed was done at Otterbourne,
  About the breaking of the day:
Earl Douglas was buried at the braken bush,
  And the Percy led captive away.

Chevy Chase

God prosper long our noble King,
    Our liffes and saftyes all!
A woefull hunting once there did
    In Chevy Chase befall.

To drive the deere with hound and horne
    Erle Pearcy took the way:
The child may rue that is unborne
    The hunting of that day!

The stout Erle of Northumberland
    A vow to God did make,
His pleasure in the Scottish woods
    Three sommers days to take;

The cheefest harts in Chevy Chase
    To kill and beare away.
These tydings to Erle Douglas came
    In Scottland where he lay,

Who sent Erle Pearcy present word
    He wold prevent his sport.
The English Erle, not fearing that,
    Did to the woods resort

With fifteen hundred bowmen bold,
    All chosen men of might,
Who knew ffull well in time of neede
    To ayme their shafts arright.

The gallant greyhound swiftly ran
　To chase the fallow deere;
On Munday they began to hunt
　Ere daylight did appeare;

And long before high noone they had
　A hundred fat buckes slaine.
Then having dined, the drovyers went
　To rouze the deare againe;

The bowmen mustered on the hills,
　Well able to endure;
Theire backsids all with speciall care
　That day were guarded sure.

The hounds ran swiftly through the woods
　The nimble deere to take,
That with their cryes the hills and dales
　An eccho shrill did make.

Lord Pearcy to the querry went
　To veiw the tender deere;
Quoth he, 'Erle Douglas promised once
　This day to meete me heere;

'But if I thought he wold not come,
　Noe longer wold I stay.'
With that a brave younge gentlman
　Thus to the Erle did say,

'Loe, yonder doth Erle Douglas come,
　Hys men in armour bright,
Full twenty hundred Scottish speres
　All marching in our sight,

'All men of pleasant Tivydale
    Fast by the river Tweede.'
'O ceaze your sportts!' Erle Pearcy said,
    'And take your bowes with speede,

'And now with me, my countrymen,
    Your courage forth advance!
For there was never champion yett
    In Scottland nor in ffrance

'That ever did on horsbacke come,
    And if my hap it were,
I durst encounter man for man,
    With him to breake a spere.'

Erle Douglas on his milke white steede,
    Most like a baron bold,
Rode formost of his company,
    Whose armour shone like gold:

'Shew me,' sayd hee, 'whose men you bee
    That hunt soe boldly heere,
That without my consent doe chase
    And kill my fallow deere.'

The first man that did answer make
    Was noble Pearcy hee,
Who sayd, 'wee list not to declare,
    Nor shew whose men wee bee,

'Yett wee will spend our deerest blood
    Thy cheefest harts to slay.'
Then Douglas swore a solempne oathe,
    And thus in rage did say,

'Ere thus I will outbraved bee,
    One of us tow shall dye!
I know thee well! an erle thou art,
    Lord Pearcy! soe am I;

'But trust me, Pearcye! pittye it were,
    And great offence, to kill
Then any of these our guiltlesse men,
    For they have done none ill;

'Let thou and I the battell trye,
    And set our men aside.'
'Accurst be [he!]' Earle Pearcye sayd,
    'By whome it is denyed.'

Then stept a gallant squire forth, –
    Witherington was his name, –
Who said, 'I wold not have it told
    To Henery our King, for shame,

'That ere my captaine fought on foote,
    And I stand looking on:
You bee two erles,' quoth Witheringhton,
    'And I a squier alone,

'Ile doe the best that doe I may,
    While I have power to stand!
While I have power to weeld my sword,
    Ile fight with hart and hand!'

Our English archers bend their bowes –
    Their harts were good and trew, –
Att the first flight of arrowes sent,
    Full foure score Scotts they slew.

43

To drive the deere with hound and horne,
    Dauglas bade on the bent;
Two captaines moved with mickle might,
    Their speres to shivers went.

They closed full fast on everye side,
    Noe slacknes there was found,
But many a gallant gentleman
    Lay gasping on the ground.

O Christ! it was great greeve to see
    How eche man chose his spere,
And how the blood out of their brests
    Did gush like water cleare!

At last these two stout erles did meet
    Like captaines of great might;
Like lyons mov'd they layd on lode,
    They made a cruell fight.

They fought, untill they both did sweat,
    With swords of tempered steele,
Till blood downe their cheekes like raine
    They trickling downe did feele.

'O yeeld thee, Pearcye!' Douglas sayd,
    'And infaith I will thee bringe
Where thou shall high advanced bee
    By James our Scottish king;

'Thy ransome I will freely give,
    And this report of thee,
Thou art the most couragious knight
    [That ever I did see].'

'No, Douglas!' quoth Erle Percy then,
    'Thy profer I doe scorne;
I will not yeelde to any Scott
    That ever yett was borne!'

With that there came an arrow keene
    Out of an English bow,
Who s[t]orke Erle Douglas on the brest
    A deepe and deadlye blow;

Who never sayd more words then these,
    'Fight on, my merrymen all!
For why, my life is att [an] end,
    Lord Pearcy sees my fall.'

Then leaving liffe, Erle Pearcy tooke
    The dead man by the hand;
Who said, 'Erle Dowglas! for thy life
    Wold I had lost my land!

'O Christ! my verry hart doth bleed
    For sorrow for thy sake!
For sure, a more redoubted knight,
    Mischance cold never take!'

A knight amongst the Scotts there was,
    Which saw Erle Douglas dye,
Who streight in hart did vow revenge
    Upon the Lord Pearcye;

SECOND PARTE

Sir Hugh Mountgomerye was he called,
    Who, with a spere full bright,
Well mounted on a gallant steed,
    Ran feircly through the fight,

And past the English archers all
    Without all dread or feare,
And through Erle Percyes body then
    He thrust his hatfull spere

With such a vehement force and might
    His body he did gore,
The staff ran through the other side
    A large cloth yard and more.

Thus did both these nobles dye,
    Whose courage none cold staine.
An English archer then perceived
    The noble Erle was slaine,

He had [a] good bow in his hand
    Made of a trusty tree:
An arrow of a cloth yard long
    To the hard head haled hee,

Against Sir Hugh Mountgomerye
    His shaft full right he sett;
The grey goose winge that was there-on,
    In his harts bloode was wett.

This fight from breake of day did last
    Till setting of the sun,
For when they rung the evening bell
    The battele scarse was done.

With stout Erle Percy there was slaine,
    Sir John of Egerton,
Sir Robert Harcliffe and Sir William,
    Sir James that bold barron;

And with Sir George and Sir James,
    Both knights of good account,
Good Sir Raphe Rebbye there was slaine,
    Whose prowesse did surmount.

For Witherington needs must I wayle
    As one in dolefull dumpes,
For when his leggs were smitten of,
    He fought upon his stumpes.

And with Erle Dowglas there was slaine
    Sir Hugh Mountgomerye,
And Sir Charles Morrell that from feelde
    One foote wold never flee;

Sir Roger Hever of Harcliffe tow, –
    His sisters sonne was hee, –
Sir David Lambwell well esteemed,
    But saved he cold not bee;

And the Lord Maxwell in like case
    With Douglas he did dye;
Of twenty hundred Scottish speeres,
    Scarce fifty-five did flye;

Of fifteen hundred Englishmen
    Went home but fifty-three;
The rest in Chevy Chase were slaine,
    Under the greenwoode tree.

Next day did many widdowes come
    Their husbands to bewayle;
They washt their wounds in brinish teares,
    But all wold not prevayle.

Theyr bodyes, bathed in purple blood,
    They bore with them away,
They kist them dead a thousand times
    Ere they were cladd in clay.

The newes was brought to Eddenborrow
    Where Scottlands King did rayne,
That brave Erle Douglas soddainlye
    Was with an arrow slaine.

'O heavy newes!' King James can say,
    'Scottland may wittenesse bee
I have not any captaine more
    Of such account as hee!'

Like tydings to King Henery came
    Within as short a space,
That Pearcy of Northumberland
    Was slaine in Chevy Chase.

'Now God be with him!' said our King,
    'Sith it will noe better bee,
I trust I have within my realme
    Five hundred as good as hee!

'Yett shall not Scotts nor Scottland say
    But I will vengeance take,
And be revenged on them all
    For brave Erle Percyes sake.'

This vow the King did well performe
    After on Humble Downe;
In one day fifty knights were slayne,
    With lords of great renowne,

And of the rest of small account,
   Did many hundreds dye:
Thus endeth the hunting in Chevy Chase
   Made by the Erle Pearcye.

God save our King, and blesse this land
   With plentye, joy, and peace;
And grant hencforth that foule debate
   Twixt noble men may ceaze!

The Sang of the Outlaw Murray

Ettricke Foreste is a feir foreste,
    In it grows manie a semelie trie;
There's hart and hynd, and dae and rae,
    And of a' wilde beastis grete plentie.

built   There's a feir castelle, bigged wi' lyme and stane;
if   O! gin it stands not pleasauntlie!
         In the forefront o' that castelle feir,
fine   Twa unicorns are bra' to see;
         There's the picture of a knight, and a ladye
             bright,
brow   And the grene hollin abune their brie.

There an Outlaw keepis five hundred men;
    He keepis a royalle companie!
His merryemen are a' in ae liverye clad,
    O' the Lincome grene saye gaye to see;
He and his ladye in purple clad,
    O! gin they lived not royallie!

Word is gane to our nobil King,
    In Edinburgh, where that he lay,
That there was an Outlaw in Ettricke Foreste,
    Counted him nought, nor a' his courtrie gay.

'I make a vowe,' then the gude King said,
    'Unto the man that deir bought me,
I shall   I'se either be King of Ettricke Foreste,
            Or King of Scotlonde that Outlaw sall be!'

50

Then spake the lord, hight Hamilton,
   And to the nobil King said he,
'My sovereign prince, sum counsell take,
   First at your nobilis, syne at me.   *then*

'I redd ye, send yon braw Outlaw till,   *advise; to*
   And see gif your man cum will he: *if*
Desyre him cum and be your man,
   And hald of you yon Foreste frie.

'Gif he refuses to do that,
   We'll conquess baith his landis and he!
Or else, we'll throw his castell down,
   And make a widowe o' his gay ladye.'

The King then call'd a gentleman,
   James Boyd (the Earle of Arran his brother
       was he);
When James he cam before the King,
   He knelit befor him on his kné.

'Wellcum, James Boyd!' said our nobil King;
   'A message ye maun gang for me;
Ye maun hye to Ettricke Foreste,
   To yon Outlaw, where bydeth he;

'Ask him of whom he haldis his landis,
   Or man, wha may his master be,
And desyre him cum, and be my man,
   And hald of me yon Foreste frie.

'To Edinburgh to cum and gang,
   His safe warrant I sall gie;

51

And gif he refuses to do that,
    We'll conquess baith his landis and he.

'Thou may'st vow I'll cast his castell down,
    And mak a widowe o' his gay ladye;
I'll hang his merryemen, payr by payr,
    In ony frith where I may them see.'

clearing

James Boyd tuik his leave o' the nobil King,
    To Ettricke Foreste feir cam he;
Down Birkendale Brae when that he cam,
    He saw the feir Foreste wi' his e'e.

Baith dae and rae, and harte and hinde,
    And of a' wilde beastis great plentie;
He heard the bows that bauldly ring,
    And arrows whidderan' hym near bi.

whizzing

Of that feir castell he got a sight;
    The like he neir saw wi' his e'e!
On the fore front o' that castell feir,
    Twa unicorns were gaye to see;
The picture of a knight, and lady bright,
    And the grene hollin abune their brie.

Thereat he spyed five hundred men,
    Shuting with bows on Newark Lee;
They were a' in ae livery clad,
    O' the Lincome grene sae gaye to see.

His men were a' clad in the grene,
    The knight was armed capapie,
With a bended bow, on a milk-white steed;
    And I wot they rank'd right bonilie.

52

Therby Boyd kend he was master man,
 And serv'd him in his ain degré.
'God mot thee save, brave Outlaw Murray!
 Thy ladye, and all thy chyvalrie!'
'Marry, thou's wellcum, gentleman,
 Some king's messenger thou seemis to be.'

'The King of Scotlonde sent me here,
 And, gude Outlaw, I am sent to thee;
I wad wot of whom ye hald your landis,
 Or man, wha may thy master be?'

'Thir landis are MINE!' the Outlaw said;
 'I ken nae King in Christentie;
Frae Soudron I this Foreste wan,   Southerner
 Whan the King nor his knightis were not
   to see.'

'He desyres you'l cum to Edinburgh,
 And hauld of him this Foreste frie;
And, gif ye refuse to do this,
 He'll conquess baith thy landis and thee.
He hath vow'd to cast thy castell down,
 And mak a widowe o' thy gaye ladye;

'He'll hang thy merryemen, payr by payr,
 In ony frith where he may them finde.'
'Ay, by my troth!' the Outlaw said,
 'Than wald I thinke me far behinde.

'Ere the King my feir countrie get,
 This land that's nativest to me!
Mony o' his nobilis sall be cauld,
 Their ladyes sall be right wearie.'

Then spak his ladye, feir of face,
  She seyd, 'Without consent of me,
That an Outlaw suld cum befor a King;
afraid I am right rad of treasonrie.
Bid him be gude to his lordis at hame,
  For Edinburgh my lord sall nevir see.'

James Boyd tuik his leave o' the Outlaw kene,
bound To Edinburgh boun is he;
When James he cam before the King,
  He knelit lowlie on his kné.

'Welcum, James Boyd!' seyd our nobil King;
  'What foreste is Ettricke Foreste frie?'
'Ettricke Foreste is the feirest foreste
  That evir man saw wi' his e'e.

'There's the dae, the rae, the hart, the hynde,
  And of a' wild beastis grete plentie;
There's a pretty castell of lyme and stane,
  O gif it standis not pleasauntlie!

'There's in the forefront o' that castell,
  Twa unicorns, sae bra' to see;
There's the picture of a knight, and a ladye bright,
  Wi' the grene hollin abune their brie.

'There the Outlaw keepis five hundred men,
  He keepis a royalle cumpanie!
His merrymen in ae livery clad,
  O' the Lincome grene sae gaye to see:
He and his ladye in purple clad;
  O! gin they live not royallie!

'He says, yon Foreste is his awin;
  He wan it frae the Southronie;
Sae as he wan it, sae will he keep it,
  Contrair all kingis in Christentie.'

'Gar warn me Perthshire, and Angus baith;   Make
  Fife up and downe, and Louthians three,
And graith my horse!' said our nobil King,   harness
  For to Ettricke Foreste hie will I me.'

Then word is gane the Outlaw till,
  In Ettricke Foreste, where dwelleth he,
That the King was cuming to his cuntrie,
  To conquess baith his landis and he.

'I mak a vow,' the Outlaw said,
  'I mak a vow, and that trulie,
Were there but three men to tak my pairt,
  Yon King's cuming full deir suld be!'

Then messengers he called forth,
  And bade them hie them speedilye –
'Ane of ye gae to Halliday,
  The Laird of the Corehead is he.

'He certain is my sister's son;
  Bid him cum quick and succour me!
The King cums on for Ettricke Foreste,
  And landless men we a' will be.'

'What news? What news?' said Halliday,
  'Man, frae thy master unto me?'
'Not as ye wad; seeking your aide;
  The King's his mortal enemie.'

55

'Aye, by my troth!' said Halliday,
 'Even for that it repenteth me;
For gif he lose feir Ettricke Foreste,
 He'll tak feir Moffatdale frae me.

'I'll meet him wi' five hundred men,
 And surely mair, if mae may be;
And before he gets the Foreste feir,
 We a' will die on Newark Lee!'

The Outlaw call'd a messenger,
 And bid him hie him speedilye,
To Andrew Murray of Cockpool —
 'That man's a deir cousin to me;
Desyre him cum, and mak me ayd,
 With a' the power that he may be.'

'It stands me hard,' Andrew Murray said,
 'Judge gif it stand na hard wi' me;
To enter against a King wi' crown,
 And set my landis in jeopardie!
Yet, if I cum not on the day,
 Surely at night he sall me see.'

To Sir James Murray of Traquair,
 A message cam right speedilye —
'What news? What news?' James Murray said,
 'Man, frae thy master unto me?'

'What neids I tell? for weel ye ken,
 The King's his mortal enemie;
And now he is cuming to Ettricke Foreste,
 And landless men ye a' will be.'

more

'And, by my trothe,' James Murray said,
  'Wi' that Outlaw will I live and die;
The King has gifted my landis lang syne —   long ago
  It cannot be nae warse wi' me.'

The King was cuming thro' Caddon Ford,
  And full five thousand men was he;
They saw the derke Foreste them before,
  They thought it awsome for to see.

Then spak the lord, hight Hamilton,
  And to the noble King said he,
'My sovereign liege, sum council tak,
  First at your nobilis, syne at me.

'Desyre him mete thee at Permanscore,
  And bring four in his cumpanie;
Five Erles sall gang yoursell befor,
  Gude cause that you suld honour'd be.

'And, gif he refuses to do that,
  We'll conquess baith his landis and he;
There sall nevir a Murray, after him,
  Hald land in Ettricke Foreste frie.'

Then spak the kene Laird of Buckscleuth,
  A stalworthye man, and sterne was he —
'For a King to gang an Outlaw till,
  Is beneath his state and his dignitie.

'The man that wons yon Foreste intill,   dwells
  He lives by reif and felonie!   plunder
Wherefor, brayd on, my sovereign liege!
  Wi' fire and sword we'll follow thee;

Or, gif your courtrie lords fa' back,
    Our Borderers sall the onset gie.'

Then out and spak the nobil King,
    And round him cast a wilie e'e –
'Now had thy tongue, Sir Walter Scott,
    Nor speik of reif nor felonie:
For, had every honeste man his awin kye,
    A right puir clan thy name wad be!'

cows

The King then call'd a gentleman,
    Royal banner-bearer there was he;
James Hop Pringle of Torsonse, by name;
    He cam and knelit upon his kné.

'Wellcum, James Pringle of Torsonse!
    A message ye maun gang for me;
Ye maun gae to yon Outlaw Murray,
    Surely where bauldly bideth he.

'Bid him mete me at Permanscore,
    And bring four in his cumpanie;
Five erles sall cum wi' mysel,
    Gude reason I suld honour'd be.

'And gif he refuses to do that,
    Bid him luke for nae good o' me!
There sall nevir a Murray, after him,
    Have land in Ettricke Foreste frie.'

James cam before the Outlaw kene,
    And serv'd him in his ain degré –
'Welcum, James Pringle of Torsonse!
    What message frae the King to me?'

'He bids ye mete him at Permanscore,
　　And bring four in your cumpanie;
Five erles sall gang himsell befor,
　　Nae mair in number will he be.

'And gif you refuse to do that,
　　(I freely here upgive wi' thee)　　　　　　avow
He'll cast yon bonny castle down,
　　And make a widowe o' that gaye ladye.

'He'll loose yon bluidhound Borderers,
　　Wi' fire and sword to follow thee;
There will nevir a Murray, after thysell,
　　Have land in Ettricke Forest frie.'

'It stands me hard,' the Outlaw said;
　　'Judge gif it stands na hard wi' me,
Wha reck not losing of mysell,
　　But a' my offspring after me.

'My merryemen's lives, my widowe's teirs –
　　There lies the pang that pinches me;
When I am straught in bluidie eard,　　　　　straight;
　　Yon castell will be right dreirie.　　　　　earth

'Auld Halliday, young Halliday,
　　Ye sall be twa to gang wi' me;
Andrew Murray, and Sir James Murray,
　　We'll be nae mae in cumpanie.'

When that they cam before the King,
　　They fell befor him on their kné –
'Grant mercie, mercie, nobil King!
　　E'en for his sake that dyed on trie.'

Such

'Sicken like mercie sall ye have;
 On gallows ye sall hangit be!'
'Over God's forbode,' quoth the Outlaw then,
 'I hope your grace will bettir be!
Else, ere you come to Edinburgh port,
 I trow thin guarded sall ye be:

'Thir landis of Ettricke Foreste feir,
 I wan them from the enemie;
Like as I wan them, sae will I keep them,
 Contrair a' kingis in Christentie.'

All the nobilis the King about,
 Said pitie it were to see him die —
'Yet graunt me mercie, sovereign prince,
 Extend your favour unto me!

'I'll give thee the keys of my castell,
 Wi' the blessing o' my gaye ladye,
Gin thou'lt make me sheriffe of this Foreste,
 And a' my offspring after me.'

'Wilt thou give me the keys of thy castell,
 Wi' the blessing of thy gaye ladye?
I'se make thee sheriffe of Ettricke Foreste,
 Surely while upwards grows the trie;
If you be not traitour to the King,

Forfeit
 Forfaulted sall thou nevir be.'

'But, Prince, what sall cum o' my men?
 When I gae back, traitour they'll ca' me.
I had rather lose my life and land,
 Ere my merryemen rebuked me.'

60

'Will your merryemen amend their lives?
    And a' their pardons I grant thee –
Now, name thy landis where'er they lie,
    And here I RENDER them to thee.'

'Fair Philiphaugh is mine by right,
    And Lewinshope still mine shall be;
Newark, Foulshiells, and Tinnies baith,
    My bow and arrow purchased me.

'And I have native steads to me,   places
    The Newark Lee and Hangingshaw;
I have mony steads in the Foreste shaw,
    But them by name I dinna knaw.'   do not

The keys o' the castell he gave the King,
    Wi' the blessing o' his feir ladye;
He was made sheriffe of Ettricke Foreste,
    Surely while upward grows the trie;
And if he was na traitour to the King,
    Forfaulted he suld nevir be.

Wha ever heard, in ony times,
    Sicken an Outlaw in his degré,
Sic favour get befor a King,
    As did the Outlaw Murray of the Foreste
        frie?

61

Johnie Armstrang

Sum speikis of lords, sum speikis of lairds,
    And sick lyke men of hie degrie;
Of a gentleman I sing a sang,
    Sum tyme called Laird of Gilnockie.

The King he wrytes a luving letter,
    With his ain hand sae tenderly,
And he hath sent it to Johnie Armstrang,
    To cum and speik with him speedily.

The Eliots and Armstrangs did convene,
    They were a gallant cumpanie —
'We'll ride and meit our lawful King,
    And bring him safe to Gilnockie.

rabbit   'Make kinnen and capon ready then,
    And venison in great plentie;
We'll wellcum here our royal King;
    I hope he'll dine at Gilnockie!'

holm   They ran their horse on the Langholme howm,
    And brak their spears wi' mickle main;
The ladies lukit frae their loft windows —
    'God bring our men weel back agen!'

When Johnie cam before the King,
    Wi' a' his men sae brave to see,
The King he movit his bonnet to him;
    He ween'd he was a King as well as he.

'May I find grace, my sovereign liege,
 Grace for my loyal men and me?
For my name it is Johnie Armstrang,
 And subject of your's, my liege,' said he.

'Away, away, thou traitor strang!
 Out o' my sight soon may'st thou be!
I grantit nevir a traitor's life,
 And now I'll not begin wi' thee.'

'Grant me my life, my liege, my King!
 And a bonny gift I'll gie to thee —
Full four and twenty milk-white steids,
 Were a' foaled in ae year to me.

'I'll gie thee a' these milk-white steids,
 That prance and nicker at a speir; neigh
And as mickle gude Inglish gilt, gold
 As four o' their braid backs dow bear.' can

'Away, away, thou traitor strang!
 Out o' my sight soon may'st thou be!
I grantit never a traitor's life,
 And now I'll not begin wi' thee!'

'Grant me my life, my liege, my King!
 And a bonny gift I'll gie to thee —
Gude four and twenty ganging mills, going
 That gang thro' a' the yeir to me.

'These four and twenty mills complete,
 Sall gang for thee thro' a' the yeir;
And as mickle of gude reid wheit, red, i.e.
 As a' their happers dow to bear.' golden
            hoppers

'Away, away, thou traitor strang!
   Out o' my sight soon may'st thou be!
I grantit nevir a traitor's life,
   And now I'll not begin wi' thee.'

'Grant me my life, my liege, my King!
   And a great gift I'll gie to thee –
Bauld four and twenty sisters' sons,
   Sall for thee fecht, tho' a' should flee!'

fight

'Away, away, thou traitor strang!
   Out o' my sight soon may'st thou be!
I grantit nevir a traitor's life,
   And now I'll not begin wi' thee.'

'Grant me my life, my liege, my King!
   And a brave gift I'll gie to thee –
All between heir and Newcastle town
   Sall pay their yeirly rent to thee.'

'Away, away, thou traitor strang!
   Out o' my sight soon may'st thou be!
I grantit nevir a traitor's life,
   And now I'll not begin wi' thee.'

'Ye lied, ye lied, now, King,' he says,
   'Altho' a King and Prince ye be!
For I've luved naething in my life,
   I weel dare say it, but honesty –

'Save a fat horse, and a fair woman,
   Twa bonny dogs to kill a deir;
But England suld have found me meal and
      mault,
   Gif I had lived this hundred yeir!

'She suld have found me meal and mault,
  And beef and mutton in a' plentie;
But nevir a Scots wyfe could have said,
  That e'er I skaithed her a puir flee.   *harmed;
                                                           poor fly*

'To seik het water beneith cauld ice,
  Surely it is a greit folie —
I have asked grace at a graceless face,
  But there is nane for my men and me!

'But had I kenn'd ere I cam frae hame,
  How thou unkind wadst been to me!
I wad have keepit the Border side,
  In spite of all thy force and thee.

'Wist England's King that I was ta'en,
  O gin a blythe man he wad be!
For anes I slew his sister's son,
  And on his breist bane brak a trie.'

John wore a girdle about his middle,
  Imbroidered ower wi' burning gold,
Bespangled wi' the same metal,
  Maist beautiful was to behold.

There hang nine targats at Johnie's hat,   *ornaments*
  And ilk ane worth three hundred pound —   *every*
'What wants that knave that a King suld have,
  But the sword of honour and the crown?

'O whair got thou these targats, Johnie,
  That blink sae brawly abune thy brie?'   *glance so
'I gat them in the field fechting,   bravely;
  Where, cruel King, thou durst not be.   brow*

'Had I my horse, and harness gude,
   And riding as I wont to be,
It suld have been tauld this hundred yeir,
   The meeting of my King and me!

Christopher   'God be with thee, Kirsty, my brother!
   Lang live thou Laird of Mangertoun!
Lang may'st thou live on the Border syde,
   Ere thou see thy brother ride up and down!

'And God be with thee, Kirsty, my son,
   Where thou sits on thy nurse's knee!
But and thou live this hundred yeir,
   Thy father's better thou'lt nevir be.

'Farewell! my bonny Gilnock hall,
   Where on Esk side thou standest stout!
Gif I had lived but seven yeirs mair,
   I wad hae gilt thee round about.'

John murder'd was at Carlinrigg,
   And all his gallant cumpanie;
But Scotland's heart was ne'er sae wae,
   To see sae mony brave men die —

Because they saved their countrey deir
   Frae Englishmen! Nane were sae bauld
While Johnie lived on the Border syde,
   Nane of them durst cum neir his hauld.

The Lochmaben Harper

O heard ye na o' the silly blind Harper,
  How lang he lived in Lochmaben town?
And how he wad gang to fair England,
  To steal the Lord Warden's Wanton Brown?

But first he gaed to his gude wyfe,
  Wi' a' the haste that he could thole —   bear, i.e.
'This wark,' quo' he, 'will ne'er gae weel,   manage
  Without a mare that has a foal.'

Quo' she — 'Thou hast a gude gray mare,
  That can baith lance o'er laigh and hie;   eap, low
Sae set thee on the gray mare's back,
  And leave the foal at hame wi' me.'

So he is up to England gane,
  And even as fast as he may drie;   bear, i.e
And when he cam to Carlisle gate,   manage
  O whae was there but the Warden, he?

'Come into my hall, thou silly blind Harper,
  And of thy harping let me hear!'
'O by my sooth,' quo' the silly blind Harper,
  'I wad rather hae stabling for my mare.'

The Warden look'd ower his left shoulder,
  And said unto his stable groom —
'Gae take the silly blind Harper's mare,
  And tie her beside my Wanton Brown.'

recited

Then aye he harped, and aye he carped,
    Till a' the lordlings footed the floor;

And further- more

But an' the music was sae sweet,
    The groom had nae mind o' the stable door.

And aye he harped, and aye he carped,
    Till a' the nobles were fast asleep;
Then quickly he took aff his shoon,
    And saftly down the stair did creep.

Then

Syne to the stable door he hied,
    Wi' tread as light as light could be;
And when he open'd and gaed in,
    There he fand thirty steeds and three.

colt

He took a cowt halter frae his hose,
    And o' his purpose he didna fail;
He slipt it ower the Wanton's nose,
    And tied it to his gray mare's tail.

He turned them loose at the castle gate,
    Ower muir and moss and ilka dale;

every

And she ne'er let the Wanton bait,
    But kept him a-galloping hame to her foal.

The mare she was right swift o' foot,
    She didna fail to find the way;
For she was at Lochmaben gate,
    A lang three hours before the day.

When she cam to the Harper's door,
    There she gave mony a nicker and sneer —

neigh; snort

'Rise up,' quo' the wife, 'thou lazy lass;
    Let in thy master and his mare.'

Then up she rose, put on her clothes,
   And keekit through at the lock-hole –   peeped
'O! by my sooth,' then cried the lass,
   'Our mare has gotten a braw brown foal!'

'Come, haud thy tongue, thou silly wench!
   The morn's but glancing in your e'e.' –
'I'll wad my hail fee against a groat,   bet my
   He's bigger than e'er our foal will be.'   whole
                                       wages

Now all this while, in merry Carlisle,
   The Harper harped to hie and law;
And the fiend dought they do but listen him to,   devil a
   Until that the day began to daw.   thing could

But on the morn, at fair day-light,
   When they had ended a' their cheer,
Behold the Wanton Brown was gane,
   And eke the poor blind Harper's mare!

'Allace! allace!' quo' the cunning auld Harper,
   'And ever allace that I cam here;
In Scotland I lost a braw cowt foal,
   In England they've stown my gude gray mare!'

'Come! cease thy allacing, thou silly blind Harper,
   And again of thy harping let us hear;
And weel payd sall thy cowt-foal be,
   And thou sall have a far better mare.'

Then aye he harped, and aye he carped;
   Sae sweet were the harpings he let them hear!
He was paid for the foal he had never lost,
   And three times ower for the gude Gray Mare.

Jamie Telfer of the Fair Dodhead

It fell about the Martinmas tyde,
    When our Border steeds get corn and hay,
The Captain of Bewcastle hath bound him
      ryde,
    And he's ower to Tividale to drive a prey.

The first ae guide that they met wi'
    It was high up in Hardhaughswire;
The second guide that they met wi',
low   It was laigh down in Borthwick water.

'What tidings, what tidings, my trusty guide?
    'Nae tidings, nae tidings, I hae to thee;
But gin ye'll gae to the fair Dodhead,
    Mony a cow's cauf I'll let thee see.'

And whan they cam to the fair Dodhead,
    Right hastily they clam the peel;
cows   They loosed the kye out, ane and a',
ransacked   And ranshackled the house right weel.

Now Jamie Telfer's heart was sair,
rolling   The tear aye rowing in his e'e;
He pled wi' the Captain to hae his gear,
    Or else revenged he wad be.

laughed The Captain turn'd him round and leugh;
    Said – 'Man, there's naething in thy house
But ae auld sword without a sheath,
kill   That hardly now wad fell a mouse.'

70

The sun wasna up, but the moon was down,
    It was the gryming of a new-fa'n snaw,   *sprinkling*
Jamie Telfer has run ten myles a-foot,
    Between the Dodhead and the Stobs's Ha'.

And whan he cam to the fair tower yate,
    He shouted loud, and cried weel hie,
Till out bespak auld Gibby Elliot –
    'Whae's this that brings the fraye to me?'

'It's I, Jamie Telfer o' the fair Dodhead,
    And a harried man I think I be!
There's naething left at the fair Dodhead,
    But a waefu' wife and bairnies three.'

'Gae seek your succour at Branksome Ha',
    For succour ye'se get nane frae me;
Gae seek your succour where ye paid black-mail,
    For, man! ye ne'er paid money to me.'

Jamie has turn'd him round about,
    I wat the tear blinded his e'e –
'I'll ne'er pay mail to Elliot again,
    And the fair Dodhead I'll never see!

'My hounds may a' rin masterless,
    My hawks may fly frae tree to tree,
My lord may grip my vassal lands,
    For there again maun I never be!'

He has turn'd him to the Tiviot side,
    E'en as fast as he could drie,   *manage*
Till he cam to the Coultart Cleuch,
    And there he shouted baith loud and hie.

Then up bespak him auld Jock Grieve –
   'Whae's this that brings the fraye to me?'
'It's I, Jamie Telfer o' the fair Dodhead,
   A harried man I trow I be.

'There's naething left in the fair Dodhead,
   But a greeting wife and bairnies three,
And sax poor ca's stand in the sta',
   A' routing loud for their minnie.'

'Alack a wae!' quo' auld Jock Grieve,
   'Alack! my heart is sair for thee!
For I was married on the elder sister,
   And you on the youngest of a' the three.'

Then he has ta'en out a bonny black,
   Was right weel fed wi' corn and hay,
And he's set Jamie Telfer on his back,
   To the Catslockhill to tak the fray.

And whan he cam to the Catslockhill,
   He shouted loud and cried weel hie,
Till out and spak him William's Wat –
   'O whae's this brings the fraye to me?'

'It's I, Jamie Telfer o' the fair Dodhead,
   A harried man I think I be!
The Captain of Bewcastle has driven my gear
   For God's sake rise, and succour me!'

'Alas for wae!' quo' William's Wat,
   'Alack, for thee my heart is sair!
I never cam by the fair Dodhead,
   That ever I fand thy basket bare.'

calves

lowing; mother

He's set his twa sons on coal-black steeds,
    Himsel' upon a freckled gray,
And they are on wi' Jamie Telfer,
    To Branksome Ha' to tak the fray.

And when they cam to Branksome Ha',
    They shouted a' baith loud and hie,
Till up and spak him auld Buccleuch,
    Said – 'Whae's this brings the fraye to me?'

'It's I, Jamie Telfer o' the fair Dodhead,
    And a harried man I think I be!
There's nought left in the fair Dodhead,
    But a greeting wife and bairnies three.'

'Alack for wae!' quoth the gude auld lord,
    'And ever my heart is wae for thee!
But fye gar cry on Willie, my son,   make
    And see that he come to me speedilie!   [them] call

'Gar warn the water, braid and wide,
    Gar warn it sune and hastilie!
They that winna ride for Telfer's kye,
    Let them never look in the face o' me!

'Warn Wat o' Harden, and his sons,
    Wi' them will Borthwick Water ride;
Warn Gaudilands, and Allanhaugh,
    And Gilmanscleugh, and Commonside.

'Ride by the gate at Priesthaughswire,
    And warn the Curors o' the Lee;
As ye cum down the Hermitage Slack,
    Warn doughty Willie o' Gorrinberry.'

The Scots they rade, the Scots they ran,
    Sae starkly and sae steadilie!

strenuously

And aye the ower-word o' the thrang
    Was – 'Rise for Branksome readilie!'

cattle

The gear was driven the Frostylee up,
    Frae the Frostylee unto the plain,
Whan Willie has look'd his men before,
    And saw the kye right fast driving.

these; did

'Whae drives thir kye?' can Willie say,

laughing-stock

    'To make an outspeckle o' me?'
'It's I, the Captain o' Bewcastle, Willie;

conceal

    I winna layne my name for thee.'

'O will ye let Telfer's kye gae back,
    Or will ye do aught for regard o' me?
Or, by the faith of my body,' quo' Willie Scott,

*I shall use;
leather*

    'I'se ware my dame's cauf's skin on thee!'

'I winna let the kye gae back,
    Neither for thy love, nor yet thy fear;
But I will drive Jamie Telfer's kye,
    In spite of every Scot that's here.'

'Set on them, lads!' quo' Willie than;
    'Fye, lads, set on them cruellie!
For ere they win to the Ritterford,

empty

    Many a toom saddle there sall be!'

Then till't they gaed, wi' heart and hand;
    The blows fell thick as bickering hail;
And mony a horse ran masterless,
    And mony a comely cheek was pale.

But Willie was stricken ower the head,
   And thro' the knapscap the sword has gane; headpiece
And Harden grat for very rage,
   Whan Willie on the grund lay slane.

But he's tane aff his gude steel cap,
   And thrice he's waved it in the air —
The Dinlay snaw was ne'er mair white
   Nor the lyart locks of Harden's hair.   streaked
                                            with grey

'Revenge! revenge!' auld Wat can cry;
   'Fye, lads, lay on them cruellie!
We'll ne'er see Tiviotside again,
   Or Willie's death revenged sall be.'

O mony a horse ran masterless,
   The splinter'd lances flew on hie;
But or they wan to the Kershope ford,   ere
   The Scots had gotten the victory.

John o' Brigham there was slane,
   And John o' Barlow, as I hear say;
And thirty mae o' the Captain's men   more
   Lay bleeding on the grund that day.

The Captain was run thro' the thick of the
        thigh,
   And broken was his right leg bane;
If he had lived this hundred year,
   He had never been loved by woman again.

'Hae back thy kye!' the Captain said;
   'Dear kye, I trow, to some they be!

if

For gin I suld live a hundred years,
    There will ne'er fair lady smile on me.'

Then word is gane to the Captain's bride,
    Even in the bower where that she lay,
That her lord was prisoner in enemy's land,
    Since into Tividale he had led the way.

rather

'I wad lourd have had a winding-sheet,
    And helped to put it ower his head,
Ere he had been disgraced by the Border Scot,
    Whan he ower Liddel his men did lead!'

Madspurs

There was a wild gallant amang us a',
    His name was Watty wi' the Wudspurs,
Cried – 'On for his house in Stanegirthside,
    If ony man will ride with us!'

banged

When they came to the Stanegirthside,
    They dang wi' trees, and burst the door;
They loosed out a' the Captain's kye,
    And set them forth our lads before.

beyond

There was an auld wyfe ayont the fire,
    A wee bit o' the Captain's kin –
'Whae dar loose out the Captain's kye,
    Or answer to him and his men?'

'It's I, Watty Wudspurs, loose the kye!
    I winna layne my name frae thee!
And I will loose out the Captain's kye,
    In scorn of a' his men and he.'

76

When they cam to the fair Dodhead,
    They were a wellcum sight to see!
For instead of his ain ten milk kye,
    Jamie Telfer has gotten thirty and three.

And he has paid the rescue shot,   reckoning
    Baith wi' goud, and white monie;
And at the burial o' Willie Scott,
    I wat was mony a weeping e'e.

77

Kinmont Willie

O have ye na heard o' the fause Sakelde?
   O have ye na heard o' the keen Lord Scroope?
How they hae ta'en bauld Kinmont Willie,
   On Hairibee to hang him up?

Had Willie had but twenty men,
   But twenty men as stout as he,
Fause Sakelde had never the Kinmont ta'en,
   Wi' eight score in his cumpanie.

They band his legs beneath the steed,
   They tied his hands behind his back;
They guarded him, fivesome on each side,
   And they brought him ower the Liddel-rack.

They led him thro' the Liddel-rack,
   And also thro' the Carlisle sands;
They brought him to Carlisle castell,
   To be at my Lord Scroope's commands.

'My hands are tied, but my tongue is free,
   And whae will dare this deed avow?
Or answer by the Border law?
   Or answer to the bauld Buccleuch!'

'Now haud thy tongue, thou rank reiver!
   There's never a Scot shall set thee free:
Before ye cross my castle yate,
   I trow ye shall take farewell o' me.'

'ear na ye that, my lord,' quo' Willie:
  'By the faith o' my body, Lord Scroope,' he said,
  I never yet lodged in a hostelrie,
  But I paid my lawing before I gaed.'   reckoning

Now word is gane to the bauld Keeper,
  In Branksome Ha', where that he lay,
That Lord Scroope has ta'en the Kinmont Willie,
  Between the hours of night and day.

He has ta'en the table wi' his hand,
  He garr'd the red wine spring on hie –   caused
'Now Christ's curse on my head,' he said,
  'But avenged of Lord Scroope I'll be!

O is my basnet a widow's curch?   helmet;
  Or my lance a wand of the willow tree?   coif
Or my arm a ladye's lilye hand,
  That an English lord should lightly me!   slight

And have they ta'en him, Kinmont Willie,
  Against the truce of Border tide?
And forgotten that the bauld Buccleuch
  Is Keeper here on the Scottish side?

'And have they e'en ta'en him, Kinmont Willie,
  Withouten either dread or fear?
And forgotten that the bauld Buccleuch
  Can back a steed, or shake a spear?

'O were there war between the lands,
  As well I wot that there is none,
I would slight Carlisle castell high,   demolish
  Tho' it were builded of marble stone.

flame
quench

'I would set that castell in a low,
    And sloken it with English blood!
There's nevir a man in Cumberland,
    Should ken where Carlisle castell stood.

'But since nae war's between the lands,
    And there is peace, and peace should be;
I'll neither harm English lad or lass,
    And yet the Kinmont freed shall be!' –

He has call'd him forty Marchmen bauld,
    I trow they were of his ain name,
Except Sir Gilbert Elliot call'd,
    The Laird of Stobs, I mean the same.

He has call'd him forty Marchmen bauld,
    Were kinsmen to the bauld Buccleuch;

armour on
shoulder

With spur on heel, and splent on spauld,
    And gleuves of green, and feathers blue.

There were five and five before them a',
    Wi' hunting horns and bugles bright;
And five and five came wi' Buccleuch,
    Like warden's men, array'd for fight:

And five and five, like a mason gang,
    That carried the ladders lang and hie;

outlaws

And five and five, like broken men;
    And so they reach'd the Woodhouselee.

And as we cross'd the Bateable Land,
    When to the English side we held,
The first o' men that we met wi',
    Whae sould it be but fause Sakelde?

'Where be ye gaun, ye hunters keen?'
  Quo' fause Sakelde; 'come tell to me!'
'We go to hunt an English stag,
  Has trespassed on the Scots countrie.'

'Where be ye gaun, ye marshal men?'
  Quo' fause Sakelde; 'come tell me true!'
'We go to catch a rank reiver,
  Has broken faith wi' the bauld Buccleuch.'

'Where are ye gaun, ye mason lads,
  Wi' a' your ladders, lang and hie?'
'We gang to herry a corbie's nest,   rob;
  That wons not far frae Woodhouselee.'   crow's
                                            lives

'Where be ye gaun, ye broken men?'
  Quo' fause Sakelde; 'come tell to me!'
Now Dickie of Dryhope led that band,
  And the never a word o' lear had he.   ore

'Why trespass ye on the English side?
  Row-footed outlaws, stand!' quo' he;   rough-shod
The nevir a word had Dickie to say,
  Sae he thrust the lance through his fause bodie.

Then on we held for Carlisle toun,
  And at Staneshaw-bank the Eden we cross'd;
The water was great and meikle of spait,   flood
  But the nevir a horse nor man we lost.

And when we reach'd the Staneshaw-bank,
  The wind was rising loud and hie;
And there the Laird garr'd leave our steeds, caused
  For fear that they should stamp and nie.

And when we left the Staneshaw-bank,
   The wind began full loud to blaw;
But 'twas wind and weet, and fire and sleet,
   When we came beneath the castle wa'.

We crept on knees, and held our breath,
   Till we placed the ladders against the wa';
And sae ready was Buccleuch himsell
   To mount the first, before us a'.

He has ta'en the watchman by the throat,
   He flung him down upon the lead —
'Had there not been peace between our land,
   Upon the other side thou hadst gaed! —

'Now sound out, trumpets!' quo' Buccleuch;
   'Let's waken Lord Scroope, right merrilie!'
Then loud the warden's trumpet blew —
   'O wha dare meddle wi' me?'

Then speedilie to work we gaed,
   And raised the slogan ane and a',
And cut a hole thro' a sheet of lead,
   And so we wan to the castle ha'.

They thought King James and a' his men
   Had won the house wi' bow and spear;
It was but twenty Scots and ten,
stir   That put a thousand in sic a stear!

sledge- Wi' coulters, and wi' forehammers,
   We garr'd the bars bang merrilie,
Untill we cam to the inner prison,
   Where Willie o' Kinmont he did lie.

And when we cam to the lower prison,
    Where Willie o' Kinmont he did lie –
'O sleep ye, wake ye, Kinmont Willie,
    Upon the morn that thou's to die?'

'O I sleep saft, and I wake aft;   *light*
    It's lang since sleeping was fleyed frae me!   *frightened*
Gie my service back to my wife and bairns,
    And a' gude fellows that spier for me.'   *ask after*

Then Red Rowan has hente him up,   *pulled*
    The starkest man in Teviotdale –   *strongest*
'Abide, abide now, Red Rowan,
    Till of my Lord Scroope I take farewell.

'Farewell, farewell, my gude Lord Scroope!
    My gude Lord Scroope, farewell!' he cried –
'I'll pay you for my lodging maill,   *rent*
    When first we meet on the Border side.'

Then shoulder high, with shout and cry,
    We bore him down the ladder lang;
At every stride Red Rowan made,
    I wot the Kinmont's airns play'd clang!   *irons*

'O mony a time,' quo' Kinmont Willie,
    'I have ridden horse baith wild and wood;   *mad*
But a rougher beast than Red Rowan,
    I ween my legs have ne'er bestrode.

'And mony a time,' quo' Kinmont Willie,
    'I've pricked a horse out oure the furs;   *furrows*
But since the day I backed a steed,
    I never wore sic cumbrous spurs!'

83

We scarce had won the Staneshaw-bank,
    When a' the Carlisle bells were rung,
And a thousand men, in horse and foot,
    Cam wi' the keen Lord Scroope along.

Buccleuch has turn'd to Eden Water,
    Even where it flow'd frae bank to brim,
And he has plunged in wi' a' his band,
    And safely swam them thro' the stream.

He turn'd him on the other side,
    And at Lord Scroope his glove flung he –
'If ye like na my visit in merry England,
    In fair Scotland come visit me!'

All sore astonish'd stood Lord Scroope,
    He stood as still as rock of stane;
trust He scarcely dared to trew his eyes,
    When thro' the water they had gane.

'He is either himsell a devil frae hell,
    Or else his mother a witch maun be;
I wad na have ridden that wan water,
    For a' the gowd in Christentie.'

Dick o' the Cow

Now Liddesdale has layen lang in,
   There is na ryding there at a';   *raiding*
The horses are a' grown sae lither fat,   *idle*
   They downa stir out o' the sta'.   *cannot*

Fair Johnie Armstrang to Willie did say —
   'Billie, a riding we will gae;   *Brother*
England and us have been lang at feid;   *feud*
   Ablins we'll light on some bootie.'   *Perhaps*

Then they are come on to Hutton Ha';
   They rade that proper place about;
But the laird he was the wiser man,
   For he had left nae gear without.   *animals*

For he had left nae gear to steal,
   Except sax sheep upon a lee:
Quo' Johnie — 'I'd rather in England die,
   Ere thir sax sheep gae to Liddesdale wi' me.   *these*

'But how ca' they the man we last met,
   Billie, as we cam owre the know?'   *knoll*
'That same he is an innocent fule,
   And men they call him Dick o' the Cow.'

'That fule has three as good kye o' his ain,   *cows*
   As there are in a' Cumberland, billie,' quo' he:
'Betide me life, betide me death,
   These kye shall go to Liddesdale wi' me.'

Then they have come on to the pure fule's house,
    And they hae broken his wa's sae wide;
They have loosed out Dick o' the Cow's three kye,
    And ta'en three co'erlets frae his wife's bed.

Then on the morn when the day was light,
    The shouts and cries rase loud and hie:
'O haud thy tongue, my wife,' he says,
    'And o' thy crying let me be!

'O, haud thy tongue, my wife,' he says,
    'And o' thy crying let me be;
And ay where thou hast lost ae cow,
    In gude suith I shall bring thee three.'

Now Dickie's gane to the gude Lord Scroope,
    And I wat a dreirie fule was he;
'Now haud thy tongue, my fule,' he says,
    'For I may not stand to jest wi' thee.'

'Shame fa' your jesting, my lord!' quo' Dickie,
    'For nae sic jesting grees wi' me;
Liddesdale's been in my house last night,
    And they hae awa my three kye frae me.

'But I may nae langer in Cumberland dwell,
    To be your puir fule and your leal,
Unless you gi' me leave, my lord,
    To gae to Liddesdale and steal.'

'I gie thee leave, my fule!' he says;
    'Thou speakest against my honour and me,
Unless thou gie me thy trowth and thy hand,
    Thou'lt steal frae nane but whae sta' frae thee.'

'There is my trowth, and my right hand!
    My head shall hang on Hairibee;
I'll ne'er cross Carlisle sands again,
    If I steal frae a man but whae sta' frae me.'

Dickie's ta'en leave o' lord and master;
    I wat a merry fule was he!
He's bought a bridle and a pair o' new spurs,
    And packed them up in his breek thie.   breech thigh

Then Dickie's come on to Pudding-burn house,
    E'en as fast as he might drie;   manage
Then Dickie's come on to Pudding-burn,
    Where there were thirty Armstrangs and three.

'O what's this come o' me now?' quo' Dickie;
    'What mickle wae is this?' quo' he;
'For here is but ae innocent fule,
    And there are thirty Armstrangs and three!'

Yet he has come up to the fair ha' board,   hall
    Sae weil he's become his courtesie!
'Weil may ye be, my gude Laird's Jock!
    But the deil bless a' your cumpanie.

'I'm come to plain o' your man, fair Johnie
        Armstrang,
    And syne o' his billie Willie,' quo' he;   next
'How they've been in my house last night,
    And they hae ta'en my three kye frae me.'

'Ha!' quo' fair Johnie Armstrang, 'we will him
        hang.'
    'Na,' quo' Willie, 'we'll him slae.'

Then up and spak another young Armstrang,
    'We'll gie him his batts, and let him gae.'

But up and spak the gude Laird's Jock,
    The best falla in a' the cumpanie,
'Sit down thy ways a little while, Dickie,
    And a piece o' thy ain cow's hough I'll gie ye.'

But Dickie's heart it grew sae grit,
    That the ne'er a bit o't he dought to eat —
Then he was aware of an auld peat-house,
    Where a' the night he thought for to sleep.

Then Dickie was aware of an auld peat-house,
    Where a' the night he thought for to lye —
And a' the prayers the puir fule pray'd,
    Were, 'I wish I had amends for my gude three
      kye!'

It was then the use of Pudding-burn house,
    And the house of Mangerton, all hail,
Them that cam na at the first ca',
    Gat nae mair meat till the neist meal.

The lads, that hungry and weary were,
    Abune the door-head they threw the key;
Dickie he took gude notice o' that,
    Says — 'There will be a bootie for me.'

Then Dickie has in to the stable gane,
    Where there stood thirty horses and three;
He has tied them a' wi' St Mary's knot,
    A' these horses but barely three.

beating *fellow* *leg* *great* *was able* *next* *hamstrung them*

88

He has tied them a' wi' St Mary's knot,
    A' these horses but barely three;
He's loupen on ane, ta'en another in hand,
    And away as fast as he can hie.

But on the morn, when the day grew light,
    The shouts and cries raise loud and hie —
'Ah! whae has done this?' quo' the gude Laird's
        Jock,
    'Tell me the truth and the verity!'

'Whae has done this deed?' quo' the gude Laird's
        Jock;
    'See that to me ye dinna lie!'
'Dickie has been in the stable last night,
    And has ta'en my brother's horse and mine frae
        me.'

'Ye wad ne'er be tald,' quo' the gude Laird's Jock;
    'Have ye not found my tales fu' leil?   _honest_
Ye ne'er wad out o' England bide,
    Till crooked, and blind, and a' would steal.'

'But lend me thy bay,' fair Johnie can say;
    'There's nae horse loose in the stable save he;
And I'll either fetch Dick o' the Cow again,
    Or the day is come that he shall die.'

'To lend thee my bay!' the Laird's Jock can say,
    'He's baith worth gowd and gude monie;
Dick o' the Cow has awa twa horse;
    I wish na thou may make him three.'

coat of mail   He has ta'en the laird's jack on his back,
        A twa-handed sword to hang by his thie;
He has ta'en a steil cap on his head,
        And gallopped on to follow Dickie.

Dickie was na a mile frae aff the town,
        I wat a mile but barely three,
When he was o'erta'en by fair Johnie Armstrang,
        Hand for hand, on Cannobie lee.

'Abide, abide, thou traitour thief!
        The day is come that thou maun die.'
Then Dickie look't owre his left shoulder,
        Said – 'Johnie, hast thou nae mae in cumpanie?

'There is a preacher in our chapell,
        And a' the live lang day teaches he:
When day is gane and night is come,
        There's ne'er ae word I mark but three.

'The first and second is – Faith and Conscience;
        The third – Ne'er let a traitour free:
But, Johnie, what faith and conscience was thine,
        When thou took awa my three kye frae me?

'And when thou had ta'en awa my three kye,
        Thou thought in thy heart thou wast not weil
           sped,
Till thou sent thy billie Willie ower the know,
        To tak thrie coverlets off my wife's bed!'

low   Then Johnie let a spear fa' laigh by his thie,
        Thought weil to hae slain the innocent, I trow;

But the powers above were mair than he,
　　For he ran but the puir fule's jerkin through.

Together they ran, or ever they blan;　　　　　stopped
　　This was Dickie the fule and he!
Dickie could na win at him wi' the blade o' the　reach
　　　　sword,
　　But fell'd him wi' the plummet under the e'e.　pommel

Thus Dickie has fell'd fair Johnie Armstrang,
　　The prettiest man in the south country —
'Gramercy!' then can Dickie say,　　　　　　did
　　'I had but twa horse, thou hast made me thrie!'

He's ta'en the steil jack aff Johnie's back,
　　The twa-handed sword that hang low by his
　　　　　thie;
He's taen the steil cap aff his head —
　　'Johnie, I'll tell my master I met wi' thee.'

When Johnie wakened out o' his dream,
　　I wat a dreirie man was he:
'And is thou gane? Now, Dickie, than
　　The shame and dule is left wi' me.　　　　sorrow

'And is thou gane? Now, Dickie, than
　　The deil gae in thy cumpanie!
For if I should live these hundred years,
　　I ne'er shall fight wi' a fule after thee.' —

Then Dickie's come hame to the gude Lord
　　　　　Scroope,
　　E'en as fast as he might hie;

'Now, Dickie, I'll neither eat nor drink,
    Till hie hanged thou shalt be.'

devil   'The shame speed the liars, my lord!' quo' Dickie;
    This was na the promise ye made to me!
For I'd ne'er gane to Liddesdale to steal,
    Had I not got my leave frae thee.'

made   'But what garr'd thee steal the Laird's Jock's
            horse?
rascal   And, limmer, what garr'd ye steal him?' quo'
            he;
'For lang thou mightst in Cumberland dwelt,
    Ere the Laird's Jock had stown frae thee.'

'Indeed I wat ye lied, my lord!
    And e'en sae loud as I hear ye lie!
I wan the horse frae fair Johnie Armstrang,
    Hand to hand, on Cannobie lee.

'There is the jack was on his back;
    This twa-handed sword hang laigh by his thie,
And there's the steil cap was on his head;
    I brought a' these tokens to let thee see.'

'If that be true thou to me tells,
    (And I think thou dares na tell a lie),
I'll gie thee fifteen punds for the horse,
    Weil tald on thy cloak lap shall be.

'I'll gie thee ane o' my best milk kye,
    To maintain thy wife and children thrie;
And that may be as gude, I think,
    As ony twa o' thine wad be.'

'The shame speed the liars, my lord!' quo' Dickie;
   'Trow ye aye to make a fule o' me?
I'll either hae twenty punds for the gude horse,
   Or he's gae to Mortan fair wi' me.'   he shall

He's gien him twenty punds for the gude horse,
   A' in goud and gude monie;
He's gien him ane o' his best milk kye,
   To maintain his wife and children thrie.

Then Dickie's come down thro' Carlisle toun,
   E'en as fast as he could drie;
The first o' men that he met wi',
   Was my lord's brother, Bailiff Glozenburrie.

'Weil be ye met, my gude Ralph Scroope!'
   'Welcome, my brother's fule!' quo' he:
'Where didst thou get fair Johnie Armstrang's
      horse?'
   'Where did I get him? but steal him,' quo' he.

'But wilt thou sell me the bonny horse?
   And, billie, wilt thou sell him to me?' quo' he: fellow
'Ay; if thou'lt tell me the monie on my cloak lap:
   For there's never ae penny I'll trust thee.'

'I'll gie thee ten punds for the gude horse,
   Weil tald on thy cloak lap they shall be;
And I'll gie thee ane o' the best milk kye,
   To maintain thy wife and children thrie.'

'The shame speid the liars, my lord!' quo' Dickie;
   'Trow ye aye to mak a fule o' me!

I'll either hae twenty punds for the gude horse,
    Or he's gae to Mortan fair wi' me.'

He's gien him twenty punds for the gude horse,
    Baith in goud and gude monie;
He's gien him ane o' his best milk kye,
    To maintain his wife and children thrie.

leapt   Then Dickie lap a loup fu' hie,
    And I wat a loud laugh laughed he —
'I wish the neck o' the third horse was broken,
    If ony of the twa were better than he!'

Then Dickie's come hame to his wife again;
    Judge ye how the puir fule had sped!
He has gien her twa score English punds,
    For the thrie auld coverlets ta'en aff her bed.

'And tak thee these twa as gude kye,
    I trow, as a' thy thrie might be;
And yet here is a white-footed nagie,
    I trow he'll carry baith thee and me.

'But I may nae langer in Cumberland bide;
    The Armstrangs they would hang me hie.'
So Dickie's ta'en leave at lord and master,
    And at Burgh under Stanmuir there dwells he.

Jock o' the Side

Now Liddesdale has ridden a raid,
    But I wat they had better hae staid at hame;
For Michael o' Winfield he is dead,
    And Jock o' the Side is prisoner ta'en.

For Mangerton house Lady Downie has gane,
    Her coats she has kilted up to her knee;
And down the water wi' speed she rins,
    While tears in spaits fa' fast frae her e'e.   *floods*

Then up and spoke our gude auld lord —
    'What news, what news, sister Downie, to me?'
'Bad news, bad news, my Lord Mangerton;
    Michael is killed, and they hae ta'en my son
           Johnie.'

'Ne'er fear, sister Downie,' quo' Mangerton;
    'I have yokes of ousen, eighty and three;   *oxen*
My barns, my byres, and my faulds a' weil fill'd, *folds*
    I'll part wi' them a' ere Johnie shall die.

'Three men I'll send to set him free,
    A' harneist wi' the best o' steil;
The English louns may hear, and drie   *rascals;*
    The weight o' their braid-swords to feel.   *endure*

'The Laird's Jock ane, the Laird's Wat twa,
    O Hobbie Noble, thou ane maun be!
Thy coat is blue, thou hast been true,
    Since England banish'd thee to me.'

Now Hobbie was an English man,
  In Bewcastle dale was bred and born:
But his misdeeds they were sae great,
  They banish'd him ne'er to return.

Lord Mangerton them orders gave,
  'Your horses the wrang way maun be shod;
Like gentlemen ye mauna seim,
  But look like corn-caugers ga'en the road.

'Your armour gude ye mauna shaw,
  Nor yet appear like men o' weir;
As country lads be a' array'd,
  Wi' branks and brecham on each mare.'

Sae now their horses are the wrang way shod,
  And Hobbie has mounted his grey sae fine;
Jock his lively bay, Wat's on his white horse
      behind,
  And on they rode for the water of Tyne.

At the Cholerford they a' light down,
  And there, wi' the help of the light o' the moon,
A tree they cut, wi' fifteen nogs on each side,
  To climb up the wa' of Newcastle toun.

But when they came to Newcastle toun,
  And were alighted at the wa',
They fand thair tree three ells ower laigh,
  They fand their stick baith short and sma'.

Then up and spak the Laird's ain Jock;
  'There's naething for't; the gates we maun
      force.'

Margin glosses: must not; -carriers; war; bridle; collar; knobs; low

But when they cam the gate untill,
    A proud porter withstood baith men and horse.

His neck in twa the Armstrangs wrang;
    Wi' fute or hand he ne'er play'd pa!   made a
His life and his keys at anes they hae ta'en,   movement
    And cast the body ahind the wa'.

Now sune they reach Newcastle jail,
    And to the prisoner thus they call;
'Sleeps thou, wakes thou, Jock o' the Side,
    Or art thou weary of thy thrall?'

Jock answers thus, wi' dulefu' tone;
    'Aft, aft I wake — I seldom sleep:
But whae's this kens my name sae weil,
    And thus to mese my waes does seik?'   soothe

Then out and spak the gude Laird's Jock,
    'Now fear ye na, my billie,' quo' he;   comrade
'For here are the Laird's Jock, the Laird's Wat,
    And Hobbie Noble, come to set thee free.'

'Now had thy tongue, my gude Laird's Jock,
    For ever, alas! this canna be;
For if a' Liddesdale were here the night,
    The morn's the day that I maun die.   Tomorrow

'Full fifteen stane o' Spanish iron,
    They hae laid a' right sair on me;
Wi' locks and keys I am fast bound
    Into this dungeon dark and dreirie.'

'Fear ye na that,' quo' the Laird's Jock;
    'A faint heart ne'er wan a fair ladie;
Work thou within, we'll work without,
    And I'll be sworn we'll set thee free.'

The first strong door that they cam at,
    They loosed it without a key;
The next chain'd door that they cam at,
made   They garr'd it a' to flinders flee.

The prisoner now upon his back,
    The Laird's Jock has gotten up fu' hie;
And down the stairs, him, irons and a',
    Wi' nae sma' speid and joy, brings he.

'Now, Jock, my man,' quo' Hobbie Noble,
    'Some o' his weight ye may lay on me.'
'I wat weil no!' quo' the Laird's ain Jock,
fly   'I count him lighter than a flee.'

Sae out at the gates they a' are gane,
    The prisoner's set on horseback hie;
way   And now wi' speid they've ta'en the gate,
every   While ilk ane jokes fu' wantonlie:

'O Jock! sae winsomely's ye ride,
    Wi' baith your feet upon ae side;
trim   Sae weel ye're harneist, and sae trig,
    In troth ye sit like ony bride!'

The night, tho' wat, they did na mind,
    But hied them on fu' merrilie,
Until they cam to Cholerford brae,
    Where the water ran like mountains hie.

But when they cam to Cholerford,
    There they met with an auld man;
Says — 'Honest man, will the water ride?
    Tell us in haste, if that ye can.'

'I wat weel no,' quo' the gude auld man;
    'I hae lived here thretty years and thrie,
And I ne'er yet saw the Tyne sae big,
    Nor running anes sae like a sea.'   once

Then out and spoke the Laird's saft Wat,
    The greatest coward in the cumpanie;
'Now halt, now halt! we need na try't;
    The day is come we a' maun die!'

'Puir faint-hearted thief!' cried the Laird's ain
        Jock,
    'There'l nae man die but him that's fie;   fated
I'll guide ye a' right safely thro';
    Lift ye the pris'ner on ahint me.'

Wi' that the water they hae ta'en,
    By ane's and twa's they a' swam thro';
'Here are we a' safe,' quo' the Laird's Jock,
    'And, puir faint Wat, what think ye now?'

They scarce the other brae had won,   bank
    When twenty men they saw pursue;
Frae Newcastle toun they had been sent,
    A' English lads baith stout and true.

But when the land-serjeant the water saw,
    'It winna ride, my lads,' says he;

Then cried aloud – 'The prisoner take,
  But leave the fetters, I pray, to me.'

'I wat weil no,' quo' the Laird's ain Jock;
  'I'll keep them a'; shoon to my mare they'll be,
My gude bay mare – for I am sure,
  She has bought them a' right dear frae thee.'

Sae now they are on to Liddesdale,
  E'en as fast as they could them hie;
The prisoner is brought to's ain fire-side,
irons   And there o's airns they mak him free.

'Now, Jock, my billie,' quo' a' the three,
  'The day is com'd thou was to die;
But thou's as weil at thy ain ingle side,
  Now sitting, I think, 'twixt thee and me.'

Hobie Noble

Foul fa the breast first treason bred in,
   That Liddisdale may safely say;
For in it there was baith meat and drink,
   And corn unto our geldings gay.

We were stout hearted men and true,
   As England it did often say:
But now we may turn our backs and fly,
   Since brave Noble is seld away.   *sold*

Now Hobie he was an English man,
   And born into Bewcastle dale;
But his misdeeds they were sae great,
   They banish'd him to Liddisdale.

At Kershope foot the tryst was set –
   Kershope of the lily lee: *lovely*
And there was traitor Sim o' the Mains,
   With him a private companie.

Then Hobie has graith'd his body weel,   *harnessed*
   I wat it was wi' baith good iron and steel;
And he has pull'd out his fringed grey,
   And there brave Noble he rade him weel.

Then Hobie is down the water gane,
   E'en as fast as he may drie;   *manage*
Tho' they shou'd a brusten and broken their   *have burst*
      hearts
   Frae that tryst Noble he would not be.

companions Weel may ye be my feiries five;
  And aye, what is your wills wi' me?
Then they cry'd a' wi' ae consent,
  Thou'rt welcome here brave Noble to me.

Wilt thou with us in England ride,
  And thy safe warrand we will be; –
If we get a horse worth a hundred punds,
  Upon his back that thou shalt be.

I dare not with you into England ride;
feud   The land-sergeant has me at feid: –
I know not what evil may betide,
  For Peter of Whitfield, his brother, is dead.

And Anton Sheil he loves not me;
droves   For twa drifts of his sheep I gat: –
The great Earl of Whitfield loves me not;
property   For nae gear frae me he e'er cou'd keep.

But will ye stay till the day gae down –
  Until the night come o'er the grund,
And I'll be a guide worth ony twa
  That may in Liddisdale be fund.

pitch Tho' dark the night as pick and tar,
  I'll lead ye o'er yon hills fu' hie;
And bring ye a' in safety back,
  If you'll be true, and follow me.

He's guided them o'er moss and muir, –
hollow   O'er hill and houp, and mony ae down;
Till they came to the Foul-bog-shiel,
  And there brave Noble he lighted down.

Then word is gane to the land-sergeant,
  In Askirtoun where that he lay:
The deer that ye hae hunted lang
  Is seen into the Waste this day. –

Then Hobie Noble is that deer,
  I wat he carries the style fu' hie.
Aft has he beat your slough-hounds back   sleuth-
  And set yourselves at little lee.   with little
                                               means of
                                               escape
Gar warn the Bows of Hartlie-Burn,   Make
  See they sharp their arrows on the wa':
Warn Willeva and spear Edom,
  And see the morn they meet me a'. –

Gar meet me on the Rodrie-haugh;
  And see it be by break o' day:
And we will on to Conscowthart Green,
  And there I think we'll get our prey. –

Then Hobie Noble has dream'd a dream,
  In the Foul-bog-sheil where that he lay:
He thought his horse was 'neath him shot,
  And he himself got hard away.

The cocks could crow and the day could dawn, did
  And I wat so even down fell the rain:
If Hobie had no waken'd at that time,
  In the Foul-bog-sheil he had been tane or
      slain.

Get up, get up, my feiries five;
  For I wat here makes a fu' ill day;

hobbler

And the warst clock of this companie,
　　I hope shall cross the Waste this day.

Now Hobie thought the gates were clear,
　　But ever alas! it was not sae;
They were beset wi' cruel men and keen,
　　That away brave Noble could not gae.

Yet follow me my feiries five,

track

　　And see of me ye keep good ray;
And the worst clock of this companie,
　　I hope shall cross the Waste this day.

There was heaps of men now Hobie before,
　　And other heaps was him behind;

strong

That had he been as wight as Wallace was,
　　Away brave Noble he could not win.

Then Hobie he had but a laddies sword,
　　But he did more than a laddies deed;
In the midst of Conscowthart green
　　He brake it o'er Jersawigham's head.

Now they have tane brave Hobie Noble,
　　Wi' his ain bow-string they band him sae:
And I wat his heart was ne'er sae sair
　　As when his ain five band him on the brae.

They have tane him for West Carlisle;
　　They ask'd him if he knew the way.
Whate'er he thought yet little he said.
　　He knew the way as well as they. —

They hae tane him up the Ricker-gate.
    The wives they cast their windows wide;
And ilka wife to anither can say,   every
    That's the man loos'd Jock o' the Side.

Fy on ye women, why ca' ye me man?
    For its nae man that I'm us'd like;
I'm but like a forfoughen hound, —   worn-out
    Has been fighting in a dirty syke.   ditch

Then they hae tane him up thro' Carlisle town,
    And set him by the chimney fire;
They gave brave Noble a wheat loaf to eat,
    And that was little his desire. —

Then they gave him a wheat loaf to eat,
    And after that a can o' beer. —
Then they cried a' wi' ae consent,
    Eat brave Noble and make good cheer.

Confess my lords horse, Hobie they say;
    And the morn in Carlisle thou's no die.   thou shalt
How shall I confess them Hobie says
    For I never saw them with mine eye.

Then Hobie has sworn a fu' great aith
    By the day that he was gotten or born,
He never had ony thing o' my lord's,
    That either eat him grass or corn.

Now fare thee weel sweet Mangerton;
    For I think again I'll ne'er the see.
I wad betray nae lad alive
    For a the goud in Christentie.

And fare thee weel now Liddisdale,
　　Baith the hie land and the law –
Keep ye weel fræ traitor Mains;
　　For goud and gear he'll sell ye a'.

property

I'd rather be ca'd Hobie Noble,
　　In Carlisle where he suffers for his faut,
Before I were ca'd traitor Mains,
　　That eats and drinks of meal and maut.

As I was a walking mine alane,   by myself
   It was by the dawning of the day,
I heard twa brithers make their mane,
   And I listened weel to what they did say.

The youngest to the eldest said,
   'Blythe and merrie how can we be?
There were three brithren of us born,
   And ane of us is condemned to die.'

'An' ye wad be merrie, an' ye wad be sad,
   What the better wad billie Archie be?   brother
Unless I had thirty men to mysell,
   And a' to ride in my cumpanie.

'Ten to hald the horses' heads,
   And other ten the watch to be,
And ten to break up the strong prison,
   Where billy Archie he does lie.'

Then up and spak him mettled John Hall
   (The luve of Teviotdale aye was he),
'An I had eleven men to mysell,
   It's aye the twalt man I wad be.'   twelfth

Then up bespak him coarse Ca'field
   (I wot and little gude worth was he),
'Thirty men is few anew,   enough
   And a' to ride in our cumpanie.'

There was horsing, horsing in haste,
    And there was marching on the lee;
Until they cam to Murraywhate,
    And they lighted there right speedilie.

'A smith! a smith!' Dickie he cries,
    'A smith, a smith, right speedilie,
calkins To turn back the caukers of our horses' shoon!
unknown   For it's unkensome we wad be.'

'There lives a smith on the water side,
    Will shoe my little black mare for me;
And I've a crown in my pocket,
    And every groat of it I wad gie.'

dark 'The night is mirk, and it's very mirk,
    And by candle-light I canna weel see;
The night is mirk, and it's very pit mirk,
drive   And there will never a nail ca' right for me.'

'Shame fa' you and your trade baith,
abet   Canna beet a gude fellow by your mystery!
blessings on But leeze me on thee, my little black mare,
    Thou's worth thy weight in gold to me.'

There was horsing, horsing in haste,
    And there was marching upon the lee;
gate Until they cam to Dumfries port,
    And they lighted there right speedilie.

'There's five of us will hold the horse,
    And other five will watchmen be:
But wha's the man, amang ye a',
gaol   Will gae to the Tolbooth door wi' me?'

O up then spak him mettled John Hall
    (Frae the laigh Tiviotdale was he),   low
'If it should cost my life this very night,
    I'll gae to the Tolbooth door wi' thee.'

'Be of gude cheir, now, Archie, lad!
    Be of gude cheir, now, dear billie!
Work thou within, and we without,
    And the morn thou'se dine at Ca'field wi'   thou shalt
       me.'

O Jockie Hall stepp'd to the door,
    And he bended low back his knee;
And he made the bolts, the door hang on,
    Loup frae the wa' right wantonlie.   Spring

He took the prisoner on his back,
    And down the Tolbooth stair cam he;
The black mare stood ready at the door,
    I wot a foot ne'er stirred she.

They laid the links out owre her neck,
    And that was her gold twist * to be;
And they cam doun thro' Dumfries toun,
    And wow but they cam speedilie.

The live lang night these twelve men rade,
    And aye till they were right wearie,
Until they came to the Murraywhate,
    And they lighted there right speedilie.

* The small gilded chains drawn across the chest of a war-
horse, as a part of his caparison. — SCOTT.

'A smith! a smith!' then Dickie he cries,
　　'A smith, a smith, right speedilie,
To file the irons frae my dear brither!
　　For forward, forward we wad be.'

They had na filed a shackle of iron,
　　A shackle of iron but barely thrie,
When out and spak young Simon brave,
　　'O dinna ye see what I do see?

'Lo! yonder comes Lieutenant Gordon,
　　Wi' a hundred men in his cumpanie;
death-
watch
Tomorrow
This night will be our lyke-wake night,
　　The morn the day we a' maun die.'

O there was mounting, mounting in haste,
　　And there was marching upon the lee;
Until they cam to Annan water,
　　And it was flowing like the sea.

shy
eddy
'My mare is young and very skeigh,
　　And in o' the weil she will drown me;
But ye'll take mine, and I'll take thine,
　　And sune through the water we sall be.'

Then up and spak him, coarse Ca'field
　　(I wot and little gude worth was he),
rest
'We had better lose ane than lose a' the lave;
　　We'll lose the prisoner, we'll gae free.'

'Shame fa' you and your lands baith!
even, i.e.
equal
　　Wad ye e'en your lands to your born billy?

110

But hey! bear up, my bonnie black mare,
    And yet thro' the water we sall be.'

Now they did swim that wan water,
    And wow but they swam bonilie!
Until they cam to the other side,
    And they wrang their cloathes right drunkily.

'Come thro', come thro', Lieutenant Gordon!
    Come thro' and drink some wine wi' me!
For there is an ale-house here hard by,
    And it shall not cost thee ae penny.'

'Throw me my irons,' quo' Lieutenant Gordon;
    'I wot they cost me dear eneugh.'
'The shame a ma,' quo' mettled John Ha',   devil a bit
    'They'll be gude shackles to my pleugh.'

'Come thro', come thro', Lieutenant Gordon!
    Come thro' and drink some wine wi' me!
Yestreen I was your prisoner,
    But now this morning am I free.'

Lord Maxwell's Goodnight

'Adieu, madame, my mother dear,
    But and my sisters three!
Adieu, fair Robert of Orchardstane!
    My heart is wae for thee.
Adieu, the lily and the rose,
    The primrose fair to see;
Adieu, my ladye, and only joy!
    For I may not stay with thee.

'Though I hae slain the Lord Johnstone,
    What care I for their feid?
My noble mind their wrath disdains:
    He was my father's deid.
Both night and day I laboured oft
    Of him avenged to be;
But now I've got what lang I sought,
    And I may not stay with thee.

'Adieu! Drumlanrig, false wert aye,
    And Closeburn in a band!
The Laird of Lag, frae my father that fled,
    When the Johnston struck aff his hand.
They were three brethren in a band —
    Joy may they never see!
Their treacherous art, and cowardly heart,
    Has twin'd my love and me.

'Adieu! Dumfries, my proper place,
    But and Carlaverock fair!

And also

feud

death

parted

112

Adieu! my castle of the Thrieve,
   Wi' a' my buildings there:
Adieu! Lochmaben's gates sae fair,
   The Langholm-holm, where birks there be; *birches*
Adieu! my ladye, and only joy,
   For, trust me, I may not stay wi' thee.

'Adieu! fair Eskdale up and down,
   Where my puir friends do dwell;
The bangisters will ding them down,   *freebooters;*
   And will them sair compell.   *beat*
But I'll avenge their feid mysell,
   When I come o'er the sea;
Adieu! my ladye, and only joy,
   For I may not stay wi' thee.'

'Lord of the land!' – that ladye said,
   'O wad ye go wi' me,
Unto my brother's stately tower,
   Where safest ye may be!
There Hamiltons, and Douglas baith,
   Shall rise to succour thee.'
'Thanks for thy kindness, fair my dame,
   But I may not stay wi' thee.'

Then he tuik aff a gay gold ring,
   Thereat hang signets three;
'Hae, take thee that, mine ain dear thing,
   And still hae mind o' me:
But, if thou take another lord,
   Ere I come ower the sea –
His life is but a three days' lease,
   Tho' I may not stay wi' thee.'

The wind was fair, the ship was clear,
    That good lord went away;
And most part of his friends were there,
    To give him a fair convey.
They drank the wine, they did na spair,
    Even in that gude lord's sight —
Sae now he's o'er the floods sae gray,
    And Lord Maxwell has ta'en his Goodnight.

Tam Lin

O I forbid you, maidens a',
    That wear gowd on your hair,
To come or gae by Carterhaugh,
    For young Tam Lin is there.

There's nane that gaes by Carterhaugh
    But they leave him a wad;   *pledge*
Either their rings, or green mantles,
    Or else their maidenhead.

Janet has belted her green kirtle,
    A little aboon her knee,
And she has broded her yellow hair
    A little aboon her bree;   *brow*
And she's awa' to Carterhaugh,
    As fast as she can hie.

When she came to Carterhaugh
    Tam Lin was at the well,
And there she fand his steed standing,
    But away was himsel.

She had na pu'd a double rose,
    A rose but only twa,
Till up then started young Tam Lin,
    Says, 'Lady, thou's pu' nae mae.   *thou shalt*

'Why pu's thou the rose, Janet,
    And why breaks thou the wand?

Or why comes thou to Carterhaugh
   Withoutten my command?'

'Carterhaugh, it is my ain,
   My daddie gave it me;
I'll come and gang by Carterhaugh
   And ask nae leave at thee.'

*

Janet has kilted her green kirtle,
   A little aboon her knee,
And she has snooded her yellow hair,
   A little aboon her bree,
And she is to her father's ha',
   As fast as she can hie.

Four and twenty ladies fair
   Were playing at the ba,
And out then cam the fair Janet,
   Ance the flower amang them a'.

Four and twenty ladies fair
   Were playing at the chess,
And out then cam the fair Janet,
   As green as onie glass.

Out then spak an auld grey knight,
   Lay o'er the castle wa',
And says, 'Alas, fair Janet, for thee,
   But we'll be blamed a'.'

'Haud your tongue, ye auld fac'd knight,
   Some ill death may ye die,

Father my bairn on whom I will,
　　I'll father nane on thee.'

Out then spak her father dear,
　　And he spak meek and mild,
'And ever alas, sweet Janet,' he says,
　　'I think thou gaes wi' child.'

'If that I gae wi' child, father,
　　Mysel' maun bear the blame;
There's ne'er a laird about your ha'
　　Shall get the bairn's name.

'If my Love were an earthly knight,
　　As he's an elfin grey,
I wadna gie my ain true-love
　　For nae lord that ye hae.

'The steed that my true-love rides on
　　Is lighter than the wind;
Wi' siller he is shod before,
　　Wi' burning gowd behind.'

Janet has kilted her green kirtle
　　A little aboon her knee;
And she has snooded her yellow hair
　　A little aboon her brie;
And she's awa to Carterhaugh
　　As fast as she can hie.

When she cam to Carterhaugh,
　　Tam Lin was at the well;
And there she fand his steed standing,
　　But away was himsel.

She had na pu'd a double rose,
    A rose but only twa,
Till up then started young Tam Lin,
    Says, 'Lady, thou pu's nae mae.

'Why pu's thou the rose, Janet,
    Amang the groves sae green,
And a' to kill the bonie babe
    That we gat us between?'

'O tell me, tell me, Tam Lin,' she says,
    'For's sake that died on tree,
If e'er ye was in holy chapel,
    Or Christendom did see?'

'Roxbrugh he was my grandfather,
    Took me with him to bide,
And ance it fell upon a day
    That wae did me betide.

'And ance it fell upon a day,
    A cauld day and a snell,
When we were frae the hunting come,
    That frae my horse I fell.
The queen o' Fairies she caught me,
    In yon green hill to dwell.

'And pleasant is the fairy-land;
    But, an eerie tale to tell!
Ay at the end of seven years
    We pay a tiend to hell.
I am sae fair and fu' o' flesh,
    I'm fear'd it be mysel'.

sharp

tithe

118

'But the night is Halloween, lady,
 The morn is Hallowday;   *Tomorrow*
Then win me, win me, an ye will,
 For weel I wat ye may.

'Just at the mirk and midnight hour *murky*
 The fairy folk will ride;
And they that wad their truelove win,
 At Milescross they maun bide.'

'But how shall I thee ken, Tam Lin,
 Or how my true love know,
Amang sae mony unco knights,   *strange*
 The like I never saw?'

'O first let pass the black, Lady,
 And syne let pass the brown;   *next*
But quickly run to the milk-white steed,
 Pu ye his rider down.

'For I'll ride on the milk-white steed,
 And ay nearest the town.
Because I was an earthly knight
 They gie me that renown.

'My right hand will be glov'd, lady,
 My left hand will be bare,
Cockt up shall my bonnet be,
 And kaim'd down shall my hair, *combed*
And thae's the takens I gie thee,
 Nae doubt I will be there.

'They'll turn me in your arms, lady,
 Into an esk and adder;   *newt*

But hold me fast and fear me not,
    I am your bairn's father.

'They'll turn me to a bear sae grim,
    And then a lion bold,
But hold me fast and fear me not,
    As ye shall love your child.

'Again they'll turn me in your arms,
    To a red het gaud of airn.
But hold me fast, and fear me not,
    I'll do to you nae harm.

bar of iron

'And last they'll turn me in your arms,
    Into the burning lead;*
Then throw me into well water,
    O throw me in wi' speed.

'And then I'll be your ain true love,
    I'll turn a naked knight.
Then cover me wi' your green mantle,
    And cover me out o' sight.'

Gloomy, gloomy was the night,
    And eerie was the way,
As fair Jenny in her green mantle
    To Milescross she did gae.

About the middle o' the night
    She heard the bridles ring;
This lady was as glad at that
    As any earthly thing.

* Perhaps 'gleed', ember.

120

First she let the black pass by,
  And syne she let the brown;
But quickly she ran to the milk-white steed,
  And pu'd the rider down.

Sae weel she minded what he did say
  And young Tam Lin did win;
Syne cover'd him wi' her green mantle
  As blythe's a bird in spring.

Out then spak the queen o' fairies,
  Out of a bush o' broom;
'Them that has gotten young Tam Lin,
  Has gotten a stately groom.'

Out then spak the queen o' fairies,
  And an angry queen was she;
'Shame betide her ill-far'd face,   ill-
  And an ill death may she die,   favoured
For she's ta'en awa' the boniest knight
  In a' my companie.

'But had I kend, Tam Lin,' she says,
  'What now this night I see,
I wad hae taen out thy twa grey een,
  And put in twa een o' tree.'   wood

The Wee Wee Man

As I was walking all alone,
  Between a water and a wa',
And there I spy'd a wee wee man,
  And he was the least that ere I saw.

His legs were scarce a shathmont's* length,
  And thick and thimber was his thighs,
Between his brows there was a span,
  And between his shoulders there was three.

heavy

He took up a meikle stane,
  And he flang't as far as I could see,
Though I had been a Wallace wight,
  I coudna liften't to my knee.

strong

O wee wee man, but thou be strong,
  O tell me where thy dwelling be?
My dwelling's down at yon' bonny bower,
  And will you go with me and see?

On we lap and awa we rade,
  Till we came to yon bonny green;
We 'lighted down for to bait our horse,
  And out there came a lady fine.

leapt

feed

Four-and-twenty at her back,
  And they were a' clad out in green,

* Measure from the point of the extended thumb to the extremity of the palm, six inches.

122

Though the King of Scotland had been there,
   The warst o' them might ha' been his queen.

On we lap and awa we rade,
   Till we came to yon bonny ha',
Where the roof was o' the beaten gould,
   And the floor was o' the crystal a'.

When we came to the stair foot,
   Ladies were dancing jimp and sma',   slender
But in the twinkling of an eye,
   My wee wee man was clean awa'.

Erlinton

Erlinton had a fair daughter,
  I wat he weird her in a great sin,
For he has built a bigly bower,
  An' a' to put that lady in.

An' he has warn'd her sisters six,
  An' sae has he her brethren se'en,
Outher to watch her a' the night,
  Or else to seek her morn an' e'en.

She hadna been i' that bigly bower,
  Na not a night but barely ane,
Till there was Willie, her ain true love,
  Chapp'd at the door, cryin', 'Peace within!'

'O whae is this at my bower door,
  That chaps sae late, or kens the gin?'
'O it is Willie, your ain true love,
  I pray you rise an' let me in!'

'But in my bower there is a wake,
  An' at the wake there is a wane;
But I'll come to the green-wood the morn,
  Whar blooms the brier by mornin' dawn.'

Then she's gane to her bed again,
  Where she has layen till the cock crew thrice,
Then she said to her sisters a',
  'Maidens, 'tis time for us to rise.'

124

She pat on her back a silken gown,
    An' on her breast a siller pin,
An' she's tane a sister in ilka hand,   each
    An' to the green-wood she is gane.

She hadna walk'd in the green-wood,
    Na not a mile but barely ane,
Till there was Willie, her ain true love,
    Whae frae her sisters has her ta'en.

He took her sisters by the hand,
    He kiss'd them baith, an' sent them hame,
An' he's ta'en his true love him behind,
    And through the green-wood they are gane.

They hadna ridden in the bonnie green-wood,
    Na not a mile but barely ane,
When there came fifteen o' the boldest knights,
    That ever bare flesh, blood, or bane.

The foremost was an aged knight,
    He wore the grey hair on his chin,
Says, 'Yield to me thy lady bright,
    An' thou shalt walk the woods within.'

'For me to yield my lady bright
    To such an aged knight as thee,
People wad think I war gane mad,
    Or a' the courage flown frae me.'

But up then spake the second knight,
    I wat he spake right boustouslie,   fiercely
'Yield me thy life, or thy lady bright,
    Or here the tane of us shall die.'   the one

earthly
mate?

'My lady is my warld's meed:
My life I winna yield to nane;
But if ye be men of your manhead,
Ye'll only fight me ane by ane.'

He lighted aff his milk-white steed,
An' gae his lady him by the head,
Say'n, 'See ye dinna change your cheer,
Until ye see my body bleed.'

oak

He set his back unto an aik,
He set his feet against a stane,
An' he has fought these fifteen men,
An' kill'd them a' but barely ane;
For he has left that aged knight,
An' a' to carry the tidings hame.

When he gaed to his lady fair,
I wat he kiss'd her tenderlie;
'Thou art mine ain love, I have thee bought;
Now we shall walk the green-wood free.'

The Twa Corbies

Ravens

As I was walking all alane,
I heard twa corbies making a mane;
The tane unto the t'other say, The one
'Where sall we gang and dine to-day?'

'In behint yon auld fail dyke, turf
I wot there lies a new-slain knight;
And nae body kens that he lies there,
But his hawk, his hound, and lady fair.

'His hound is to the hunting gane,
His hawk to fetch the wild-fowl hame,
His lady's ta'en another mate,
So we may make our dinner sweet.

'Ye'll sit on his white hause bane, neck
And I'll pike out his bonny blue een:
Wi' ae lock o' his gowden hair,
We'll theek our nest when it grows bare. thatch

'Mony a one for him makes mane,
But nane sall ken whare he is gane:
O'er his white banes, when they are bare,
The wind sall blaw for evermair.'

The Douglas Tragedy

'Rise up, rise up, now, Lord Douglas,' she says,
   'And put on your armour so bright;
Let it never be said that a daughter of thine
   Was married to a lord under night.

'Rise up, rise up, my seven bold sons,
   And put on your armour so bright,
And take better care of your youngest sister,
   For your eldest's awa the last night.'

He's mounted her on a milk-white steed,
   And himself on a dapple grey,
With a bugelet horn hung down by his side,
   And lightly they rode away.

Lord William lookit o'er his left shoulder,
   To see what he could see,
And there he spy'd her seven brethren bold,
   Come riding over the lee.

'Light down, light down, Lady Marg'ret,' he said,
   'And hold my steed in your hand,
Until that against your seven brethren bold,
   And your father, I mak a stand.'

She held his steed in her milk-white hand,
   And never shed one tear,
Until that she saw her seven brethren fa',
   And her father hard fighting, who lov'd her so
      dear.

'O hold your hand, Lord William!' she said,
  'For your strokes they are wond'rous sair;
True lovers I can get many a ane,
  But a father I can never get mair.'

O she's ta'en out her handkerchief,
  It was o' the holland sae fine,
And aye she dighted her father's bloody wounds,   wiped
  That were redder than the wine.

'O chuse, O chuse, Lady Marg'ret,' he said,
  'O whether will ye gang or bide?'
'I'll gang, I'll gang, Lord William,' she said,
  'For ye have left me no other guide.'

He's lifted her on a milk-white steed,
  And himself on a dapple grey,
With a bugelet horn hung down by his side,
  And slowly they baith rade away.

O they rade on, and on they rade,
  And a' by the light of the moon,
Until they came to yon wan water,
  And there they lighted down.

They lighted down to tak a drink
  Of the spring that ran sae clear;
And down the stream ran his gude heart's
      blood,
  And sair she gan to fear.

'Hold up, hold up, Lord William,' she says,
  'For I fear that you are slain!'

"'Tis naething but the shadow of my scarlet
  cloak,
  That shines in the water sae plain.'

O they rade on, and on they rade,
  And a' by the light of the moon,
Until they cam to his mother's ha' door,
  And there they lighted down.

'Get up, get up, lady mother,' he says,
  'Get up, and let me in! –
Get up, get up, lady mother,' he says,
  'For this night my fair lady I've win.

'O mak my bed, lady mother,' he says,
  'O mak it braid and deep!
And lay Lady Marg'ret close at my back,
  And the sounder I will sleep.'

Lord William was dead lang ere midnight,
  Lady Marg'ret lang ere day –
And all true lovers that go thegither,
  May they have mair luck than they!

Lord William was buried in St Marie's kirk,
  Lady Margaret in Marie's quire;
Out o' the lady's grave grew a bonny red rose,
  And out o' the knight's a brier.

intertwined   And they twa met, and they twa plat,
  And fain they wad be near;
And a' the warld might ken right weel,
  They were twa lovers dear.

But bye and rade the Black Douglas,
    And wow but he was rough!
For he pull'd up the bonny brier,
    And flang'd in St Mary's Loch.

Young Benjie

Of a' the maids o' fair Scotland,
   The fairest was Marjorie;
And young Benjie was her ae true love,
   And a dear true love was he.

And wow! but they were lovers dear,
   And loved fu' constantlie;
But aye the mair when they fell out,
quarrel   The sairer was their plea.

And they hae quarrell'd on a day,
   Till Marjorie's heart grew wae;
And she said she'd chuse another luve,
   And let young Benjie gae.

stubborn   And he was stout, and proud-hearted,
   And thought o't bitterlie;
And he's gane by the wan moon-light,
   To meet his Marjorie.

'O open, open, my true love,
   O open, and let me in!'
'I dare na open, young Benjie,
   My three brothers are within.'

maid   'Ye lied, ye lied, ye bonny burd,
   Sae loud's I hear ye lie;
As I came by the Lowden banks,
   They bade gude e'en to me.

'But fare ye weel, my ae fause love,
   That I have loved sae lang!
It sets ye chuse another love,   becomes
   And let young Benjie gang.'   you

Then Marjorie turn'd her round about,
   The tear blinding her ee, —
'I darena, darena, let thee in,
   But I'll come down to thee.'

Then saft she smiled, and said to him,
   'O what ill hae I done?'
He took her in his armis twa,
   And threw her o'er the linn.

The stream was strang, the maid was stout,
   And laith laith to be dang,   loath;
But, ere she wan the Lowden banks,   beaten
   Her fair colour was wan.

Then up bespak her eldest brother,
   'O see na ye what I see?'
And out then spak her second brother,
   'It's our sister Marjorie!'

Out then spak her eldest brother,
   'O how shall we her ken?'
And out then spak her youngest brother,
   'There's a honey mark on her chin.'   mole

Then they've ta'en up the comely corpse,
   And laid it on the ground —
'O wha has killed our ae sister,
   And how can he be found?

death-
watch

'The night it is her low lykewake,
  The morn her burial day,

dark

And we maun watch at mirk midnight,
  And hear what she will say.'

Wi' doors ajar, and candle light,
  And torches burning clear,

laid out

The streikit corpse, till still midnight,
  They waked, but naething hear.

About the middle o' the night,
  The cocks began to craw;
And at the dead hour o' the night,

twist

  The corpse began to thraw.

'O whae has done the wrang, sister,
  Or dared the deadly sin?
Whae was sae stout, and fear'd nae dout,
  As thraw ye o'er the linn?'

'Young Benjie was the first ae man
  I laid my love upon;
He was sae stout, and proud-hearted,
  He threw me o'er the linn.'

'Sall we young Benjie head, sister,
  Sall we young Benjie hang,
Or sall we pike out his twa gray een,
  And punish him ere he gang?'

'Ye mauna Benjie head, brothers,
  Ye mauna Benjie hang,
But ye maun pike out his twa gray een,
  And punish him ere he gang.

'Tie a green gravat round his neck,   cravat
   And lead him out and in,
And the best ae servant about your house
   To wait young Benjie on.

'And aye, at every seven years' end,
   Ye'll tak him to the linn;
For that's the penance he maun drie,   bear
   To scug his deadly sin.'   expiate

Fine Flowers in the Valley

She sat down below a thorn,
    Fine flowers in the valley,
And there she has her sweet babe born,
    And the green leaves they grow rarely.

Smile na sae sweet, my bonie babe,
    Fine flowers in the valley,
And ye smile sae sweet, ye'll smile me dead,
    And the green leaves they grow rarely.

She's taen out her little penknife,
    Fine flowers in the valley,
deprived   And twinn'd the sweet babe o' its life,
    And the green leaves they grow rarely.

dug   She's howket a grave by the light o' the moon,
    Fine flowers in the valley,
And there she's buried her sweet babe in,
    And the green leaves they grow rarely.

As she was going to the church,
    Fine flowers in the valley,
She saw a sweet babe in the porch,
    And the green leaves they grow rarely.

if   O sweet babe and thou were mine,
    Fine flowers in the valley,
I wad cleed thee in the silk so fine,
    And the green leaves they grow rarely.

O mother dear, when I was thine,
   Fine flowers in the valley,
You did na prove to me sae kind,
   And the green leaves they grow rarely.

The Broomfield Hill

There was a knight and a lady bright
    Had a true tryst at the broom;
The ane ga'ed early in the morning,
    The other in the afternoon.

And aye she sat in her mother's bower door,
    And aye she made her mane,
'Oh whether should I gang to the Broomfield
    hill,
    Or should I stay at hame?

'For if I gang to the Broomfield hill,
    My maidenhead is gone;
And if I chance to stay at hame,
    My love will ca' me mansworn.'

Up then spake a witch woman,
    Aye from the room aboon;
'O, ye may gang to Broomfield hill,
    And yet come maiden hame.

'For, when ye gang to the Broomfield hill,
    Ye'll find your love asleep,
With a silver-belt about his head,
    And a broom-cow at his feet.

'Take ye the blossom of the broom,
    The blossom it smells sweet,
And strew it at your true love's head,
    And likewise at his feet.

138

'Take ye the rings off your fingers,
　　Put them on his right hand,
To let him know, when he doth awake,
　　His love was at his command.'

She pu'd the broom flower on Hive-hill,
　　And strew'd on's white hals bane,　　　　neck
And that was to be wittering true,　　　　indication
　　That maiden she had gane.

'O where were ye, my milk-white steed,
　　That I hae coft sae dear,　　　　bought
That wadna watch and waken me,
　　When there was maiden here?'

'I stamped wi' my foot, master,
　　And gar'd my bridle ring;　　　　made
But nae kin' thing wald waken ye,
　　Till she was past and gane.'

'And wae betide ye, my gay goss hawk,
　　That I did love sae dear,
That wadna watch and waken me,
　　When there was maiden here.'

'I clapped wi' my wings, master,
　　And aye my bells I rang,
And aye cry'd, Waken, waken, master,
　　Before the ladye gang.'

'But haste and haste, my gude white steed,
　　To come the maiden till,
Or a' the birds of gude green wood
　　Of your flesh shall have their fill.'

'Ye needna burst your gude white steed,
   Wi' racing o'er the howm;
Nae bird flies faster through the wood,
   Than she fled through the broom.'

holm

Proud Lady Margaret

'Twas on a night, an evening bright,
    When the dew began to fa',
Lady Margaret was walking up and down,
    Looking o'er her castle wa'.

She looked east, and she looked west,
    To see what she could spy,
When a gallant knight came in her sight,
    And to the gate drew nigh.

'You seem to be no gentleman,
    You wear your boots so wide;
But you seem to be some cunning hunter,
    You wear the horn so syde.'   **low**

'I am no cunning hunter,' he said,
    'Nor ne'er intend to be;
But I am come to this castle
    To seek the love of thee;
And if you do not grant me love,
    This night for thee I'll die.'

'If you should die for me, sir knight,
    There's few for you will mane,
For mony a better has died for me,
    Whose graves are growing green.

'But ye maun read my riddle,' she said,
    'And answer my questions three;

And but ye read them right,' she said,
  'Gae stretch ye out and die. –

'Now what is the flower, the ae first flower,
  Springs either on moor or dale?
And what is the bird, the bonnie bonnie bird,
  Sings on the evening gale?'

'The primrose is the ae first flower
  Springs either on moor or dale;
And the thistlecock is the bonniest bird
  Sings on the evening gale.'

'But what's the little coin,' she said,
  'Wald buy my castle bound?
And what's the little boat,' she said,
  'Can sail the world all round?'

'O hey, how mony small pennies
  Make thrice three thousand pound?
Or hey, how mony small fishes
  Swim a' the salt sea round?'

'I think ye maun be my match,' she said,
  'My match, and something mair,
You are the first e'er got the grant
  Of love frae my father's heir.

'My father was lord of nine castles,
  My mother lady of three;
My father was lord of nine castles,
  And there's nane to heir but me.

'And round about a' thae castles,
    You may baith plow and saw,
And on the fifteenth day of May,
    The meadows they will maw.'

'O hald your tongue, Lady Margeret,' he said,
    'For loud I hear you lie!
Your father was lord of nine castles,
    Your mother was lady of three;
Your father was lord of nine castles,
    But ye fa' heir to but three.

'And round about a' thae castles,
    You may baith plow and saw,
But on the fifteenth day of May
    The meadows will not maw.

'I am your brother Willie,' he said,
    'I trow ye ken na me;
I came to humble your haughty heart,
    Has gar'd sae mony die.'   made

'If ye be my brother Willie,' she said,
    'As I trow weel ye be,
This night I'll neither eat nor drink,
    But gae alang wi' thee.'

'O hald your tongue, Lady Margaret,' he said,
    'Again I hear you lie;
For ye've unwashen hands, and ye've unwashen
        feet,*
    To gae to clay wi' me.

* *Unwashen hands and unwashen feet* – Alluding to the custom of washing and dressing dead bodies. – SCOTT.

143

'For the wee worms are my bedfellows,
    And cauld clay is my sheets;
And when the stormy winds do blow,
    My body lies and sleeps.'

The Broom of Cowdenknows

O the broom, and the bonny bonny broom,
   And the broom of the Cowdenknows!
And aye sae sweet as the lassie sang,
   I' the bought, milking the ewes.   fold

The hills were high on ilka side,   every
   An' the bought i' the lirk o' the hill,   hollow
And aye, as she sang, her voice it rang,
   Out o'er the head o' yon hill.

There was a troop o' gentlemen
   Came riding merrilie by,
And one of them has rode out o' the way,
   To the bought to the bonny may.   maid

'Weel may ye save an' see, bonny lass,
   An' weel may ye save an' see.'
'An' sae wi' you, ye weel-bred knight,
   And what's your will wi' me?'

'The night is misty and mirk, fair may,   murky
   And I have ridden astray,
And will ye be so kind, fair may,
   As come out and point my way?'

'Ride out, ride out, ye ramp rider!   riotous
   Your steed's baith stout and strang;
For out of the bought I dare na come,
   For fear 'at ye do me wrang.'

145

'O winna ye pity me, bonny lass,
      O winna ye pity me?
An' winna ye pity my poor steed,
      Stands trembling at yon tree?'

'I wadna pity your poor steed,
      Tho' it were tied to a thorn;
For if ye wad gain my love the night,
      Ye wad slight me ere the morn.

-decked

'For I ken you by your weel-busked hat,
      And your merrie twinkling e'e,
That ye're the Laird o' the Oakland hills,
      An' ye may weel seem for to be.'

'But I am not the Laird o' the Oakland hills,
      Ye're far mista'en o' me;
But I'm ane o' the men about his house
      An' right aft in his companie.'

slender

He's ta'en her by the middle jimp,
      And by the grass-green sleeve;

fold-wall
asked

He's lifted her over the fauld dyke,
      And speer'd at her sma' leave.

O he's ta'en out a purse o' gowd,

stroked

      And streek'd her yellow hair,
'Now, take ye that, my bonnie may,
      Of me till you hear mair.'

O he's leapt on his berry-brown steed,
      An' soon he's o'erta'en his men;
And ane and a' cried out to him,
      'O master, ye've tarry'd lang!'

'O I hae been east, and I hae been west,
   An' I hae been far o'er the knowe,   knoll
But the bonniest lass that ever I saw
   Is i' the bought milking the ewes.'

She set the cog upon her head,   milking-
   An' she's gane singing hame —   pail
'O where hae ye been, my ae daughter?
   Ye hae na been your lane.'   by yourself

'O nae body was wi' me, father,
   O nae body has been wi' me;
The night is misty and mirk, father,
   Ye may gang to the door and see.

'But wae be to your ewe-herd, father,
   And an ill deed may he die;
He bug the bought at the back o' the knowe,   built
   And a tod has frighted me.   fox

'There came a tod to the bought-door,
   The like I never saw;
And ere he had tane the lamb he did,
   I had lourd he had ta'en them a'.'   rather

O whan fifteen weeks was come and gane,
   Fifteen weeks and three,
That lassie began to look thin and pale,
   An' to long for his merry twinkling e'e.

It fell on a day, on a het simmer day,
   She was ca'ing out her father's kye,   driving;
Bye came a troop o' gentlemen,   cows
   A' merrilie riding bye.

'Weel may ye save an' see, bonny may,
  Weel may ye save and see!
Weel I wat, ye be a very bonny may,
  But whae's aught that babe ye are wi'?'

*who is
it owns*

Never a word could that lassie say,
  For never a ane could she blame,
An' never a word could the lassie say,
  But 'I have a gudeman at hame.'

'Ye lied, ye lied, my very bonny may,
  Sae loud as I hear you lie;
For dinna ye mind that misty night
  I was i' the bought wi' thee?

'I ken you by your middle sae jimp,
  An' your merry twinkling e'e,
That ye're the bonny lass i' the Cowdenknow,
  An' ye may weel seem for to be.'

Then he's leapt off his berry-brown steed,
  An' he's set that fair may on –
Ca' out your kye, gude father, yoursell,
  For she's never ca' them out again.

'I am the Laird of the Oakland hills,
  I hae thirty plows and three;
An' I hae gotten the bonniest lass
  That's in a' the south countrie.'

Lord Randal

'O where hae ye been, Lord Randal, my son?
O where hae ye been, my handsome young man?'
'I hae been to the wild wood; mother, make my bed
    soon,
For I'm weary wi' hunting, and fain wald lie down.'

'Where gat ye your dinner, Lord Randal, my son?
Where gat ye your dinner, my handsome young man?'
'I din'd wi' my true-love; mother, make my bed soon,
For I'm weary wi' hunting, and fain wald lie down.'

'What gat ye to your dinner, Lord Randal, my son?
What gat ye to your dinner, my handsome young
    man?'
'I gat eels boil'd in broo'; mother, make my bed soon, broth
For I'm weary wi' hunting, and fain wald lie down.'

'What became of your bloodhounds, Lord Randal,
    my son?
What became of your bloodhounds, my handsome
    young man?'
'O they swell'd and they died; mother, make my bed
    soon,
For I'm weary wi' hunting, and fain wald lie down.'

'O I fear ye are poison'd, Lord Randal, my son!
O I fear ye are poison'd, my handsome young man!'
'O yes! I am poison'd; mother, make my bed soon,
For I'm sick at the heart, and I fain wald lie down.'

Sir Hugh le Blond

The birds sang sweet as ony bell,
 The world had not their make,
The Queen she's gone to her chamber,
 With Rodingham to talk.

match

'I love you well, my Queen, my dame,
 'Bove land and rents so clear,
And for the love of you, my Queen,
 Would thole pain most severe.'

bear

'If well you love me, Rodingham,
 I'm sure so do I thee:
I love you well as any man,
 Save the King's fair bodye.'

'I love you well, my Queen, my dame;
 'Tis truth that I do tell:
And for to lye a night with you,
 The salt seas I would sail.'

'Away, away, O Rodingham!
 You are both stark and stoor;
Would you defile the King's own bed,
 And make his Queen a whore,

arrant;
rough

'Tomorrow you'd be taken sure,
 And like a traitor slain;
And I'd be burned at a stake,
 Altho' I be the Queen.'

He then stepp'd out at her room-door,
   All in an angry mood:
Until he met a leper-man,
   Just by the hard way-side.

He intoxicate the leper-man
   With liquors very sweet;
And gave him more and more to drink,
   Until he fell asleep.

He took him in his arms two,
   And carried him along,
Till he came to the Queen's own bed,
   And there he laid him down.

He then stepp'd out of the Queen's bower,
   As swift as any roe,
'Till he came to the very place
   Where the King himself did go.

The King said unto Rodingham,
   'What news have you to me?'
He said, 'Your Queen's a false woman,
   As I did plainly see.'

He hasten'd to the Queen's chamber,
   So costly and so fine,
Until he came to the Queen's own bed,
   Where the leper-man was lain.

He looked upon the leper-man,
   Who lay on his Queen's bed;
He lifted up the snaw-white sheets,
   And thus he to him said:

'Plooky, plooky are your cheeks,
    And plooky is your chin,
And plooky are your arms two
    My bonny Queen's layne in.

Pimply

'Since she has lain into your arms,
    She shall not lye in mine;
Since she has kiss'd your ugsome mouth,
    She never shall kiss mine.'

ghastly

In anger he went to the Queen,
    Who fell upon her knee;
He said, 'You false, unchaste woman,
    What's this you've done to me?'

The Queen then turn'd herself about,
    The tear blinded her e'e –
'There's not a knight in a' your court
    Dare give that name to me.'

He said ''Tis true that I do say;
    For I a proof did make:
You shall be taken from my bower,
    And burned at a stake.

'Perhaps I'll take my word again,
    And may repent the same,
If that you'll get a Christian man
    To fight that Rodingham.'

'Alas! alas!' then cried our Queen,
    'Alas, and woe to me!
There's not a man in all Scotland
    Will fight with him for me.'

She breathed unto her messengers,
    Sent them south, east, and west;
They could find none to fight with him,
    Nor enter the contest.

She breathed on her messengers,
    She sent them to the north;
And there they found Sir Hugh le Blond,
    To fight him he came forth.

When unto him they did unfold
    The circumstance all right,
He bade them go and tell the Queen,
    That for her he would fight.

The day came on that was to do
    That dreadful tragedy;
Sir Hugh le Blond was not come up
    To fight for our ladye.

'Put on the fire,' the monster said;
    'It is twelve on the bell.'
''Tis scarcely ten, now,' said the King;
    'I heard the clock mysell.'

Before the hour the Queen is brought,
    The burning to proceed;
In a black velvet chair she's set,
    A token for the dead.

She saw the flames ascending high,
    The tears blinded her e'e;
'Where is the worthy knight,' she said,
    'Who is to fight for me?'

Then up and spak the King himsel,
    'My dearest, have no doubt,
For yonder comes the man himsel,
    As bold as e'er set out.'

They then advanced to fight the duel
    With swords of temper'd steel,
Till down the blood of Rodingham
    Came running to his heel.

Sir Hugh took out a lusty sword,
    'Twas of the metal clear;
And he has pierced Rodingham
    Till's heart-blood did appear.

'Confess your treachery, now,' he said,
    'This day before you die!'
'I do confess my treachery,
    I shall no longer lye:

'I like to wicked Haman am,
    This day I shall be slain.'
The Queen was brought to her chamber,
    A good woman again.

The Queen then said unto the King,
    'Arbattle's near the sea;
Give it unto the northern knight,
    That this day fought for me.'

Then said the King, 'Come here, Sir Knight,
    And drink a glass of wine;
And, if Arbattle's not enough,
    To it we'll Fordoun join.'

Græme and Bewick

Gude Lord Græme is to Carlisle gane;
   Sir Robert Bewick there met he;
And arm in arm to the wine they did go,
   And they drank till they were baith merrie.

Gude Lord Græme has ta'en up the cup,
   'Sir Robert Bewick, and here's to thee!
And here's to our twae sons at hame!
   For they like us best in our ain countrie.'

'O were your son a lad like mine,
   And learn'd some books that he could read,
They might have been twae brethren bauld,
   And they might hae bragged the Border side.'   defied

'But your son's a lad, and he is but bad,
   And billie to my son he canna be;   brother

       *

'Ye sent him to the schools, and he wadna learn;
   Ye bought him books, and he wadna read.' –
'But my blessing shall he never earn,
   Till I see how his arm can defend his head.'

Gude Lord Græme has a reckoning call'd,
   A reckoning then called he;
And he paid a crown, and it went roun';
   It was all for the gude wine and free.

And he has to the stable ga'en,
   Where there stude thirty steeds and three;
He's ta'en his ain horse amang them a',
   And hame he rade sae manfullie.

'Wellcome, my auld father!' said Christie Græme,
   'But where sae lang frae hame were ye?'
'It's I hae been at Carlisle town,
   And a baffled man by thee I be.

'I hae been at Carlisle town,
   Where Sir Robert Bewick he met me;
He says ye're a lad, and ye are but bad,
   And billie to his son ye canna be.

'I sent ye to the schools, and ye wadna learn;
   I bought ye books, and ye wadna read;
Therefore my blessing ye shall never earn,
   Till I see with Bewick thou save thy head.'

'Now, God forbid, my auld father,
   That ever sic a thing suld be!
Billie Bewick was my master, and I was his
     scholar,
   And aye sae weel as he learned me.'

rascal   'O hald thy tongue, thou limmer loon,
   And of thy talking let me be!
If thou does na end me this quarrel soon,
   There is my glove I'll fight wi' thee.'

Then Christie Græme he stooped low
   Unto the ground, you shall understand; —

'O father, put on your glove again,
    The wind has blown it from your hand.'

'What's that thou says, thou limmer loon?
    How dares thou stand to speak to me?
If thou do not end this quarrel soon,
    There's my right hand thou shalt fight with me.'

Then Christie Græme's to his chamber gane,
    To consider weel what then should be;
Whether he suld fight with his auld father,
    Or with his billie Bewick, he.

'If I suld kill my billie dear,
    God's blessing I shall never win;
But if I strike at my auld father,
    I think 'twald be a mortal sin.

'But if I kill my billie dear,
    It is God's will! so let it be.
But I make a vow, ere I gang frae hame,
    That I shall be the next man's die.'

Then he's put on's back a gude ould jack,   jacket
    And on his head a cap of steel,
And sword and buckler by his side;
    O gin he did not become them weel!

We'll leave off talking of Christie Græme,
    And talk of him again belive;   soon
And we will talk of bonny Bewick,
    Where he was teaching his scholars five.

157

When he had taught them well to fence,
    And handle swords without any doubt,
He took his sword under his arm,
    And he walk'd his father's close about.

He looked atween him and the sun,
    And a' to see what there might be,
Till he spied a man in armour bright,
    Was riding that way most hastilie.

'O wha is yon, that came this way,
    Sae hastilie that hither came?
I think it be my brother dear;
    I think it be young Christie Græme. –

'Ye're welcome here, my billie dear,
    And thrice ye're welcome unto me!'
'But I'm wae to say, I've seen the day,
    When I am come to fight wi' thee.

'My father's gane to Carlisle town,
    Wi' your father Bewick there met he;
He says I'm a lad, and I am but bad,
    And a baffled man I trow I be.

'He sent me to schools, and I wadna learn;
    He gae me books, and I wadna read;
Sae my father's blessing I'll never earn,
    Till he see how my arm can guard my head.'

'O God forbid, my billie dear,
    That ever such a thing suld be!
We'll take three men on either side,
    And see if we can our fathers agree.'

'O hald thy tongue, now, billie Bewick,
    And of thy talking let me be!
But if thou'rt a man, as I'm sure thou art,
    Come o'er the dyke, and fight wi' me.'

'But I hae nae harnesse, billie, on my back,
    As weel I see there is on thine.'
'But as little harness as is on thy back,
    As little, billie, shall be on mine.'

Then he's thrown aff his coat of mail,
    His cap of steel away flung he;
He stuck his spear into the ground,
    And he tied his horse unto a tree.

Then Bewick has thrown aff his cloak,
    And's psalter-book frae's hand flung he;
He laid his hand upon the dyke,
    And ower he lap most manfullie.

O they hae fought for twae lang hours;
    When twae lang hours were come and gane,
The sweat drapp'd fast frae aff them baith,
    But a drap of blude could not be seen

Till Græme gae Bewick an ackward stroke,   backward
    Ane ackward stroke strucken sickerlie;   surely
He has hit him under the left breast,
    And dead-wounded to the ground fell he.

'Rise up, rise up, now, billie dear!
    Arise, and speak three words to me! —
Whether thou's gotten thy deadly wound,
    Or if God and good leaching may succour thee?'

'O horse, O horse, now billie Græme,
    And get thee far from hence with speed;
And get thee out of this country,
    That none may know who has done the deed.'

'O I have slain thee, billie Bewick,
    If this be true thou tellest to me;
But I made a vow, ere I came frae hame,
    That aye the next man I wad be.'

mole hill   He has pitch'd his sword in a moodie-hill,
    And he has leap'd twenty lang feet and three,
And on his ain sword's point he lap,
    And dead upon the ground fell he.

'Twas then came up Sir Robert Bewick,
    And his brave son alive saw he;
'Rise up, rise up, my son,' he said,
    'For I think ye hae gotten the victorie.'

'O hald your tongue, my father dear!
    Of your prideful talking let me be!
Ye might hae drunken your wine in peace,
    And let me and my billie be.

'Gae dig a grave, baith wide and deep,
    And a grave to hald baith him and me;
But lay Christie Græme on the sunny side,
    For I'm sure he wan the victorie.'

'Alack! a wae!' auld Bewick cried,
    'Alack! was I not much to blame!
I'm sure I've lost the liveliest lad
    That e'er was born unto my name.'

'Alack! a wae!' quo' gude Lord Græme,
   'I'm sure I hae lost the deeper lack!
I durst hae ridden the Border through,
   Had Christie Græme been at my back.

'Had I been led through Liddesdale,
   And thirty horsemen guarding me,
And Christie Græme been at my back,
   Sae soon as he had set me free!

'I've lost my hopes, I've lost my joy,
   I've lost the key but and the lock;   as well as
I durst hae ridden the world round,
   Had Christie Græme been at my back.'

The Lament of the Border Widow

My love he built me a bonny bower,
And clad it a' wi' lilye flour,
A brawer bower ye ne'er did see,
Than my true love he built for me.

finer

There came a man, by middle day,
He spied his sport, and went away;
And brought the King that very night,
Who brake my bower, and slew my knight.

He slew my knight, to me sae dear;
He slew my knight, and poin'd his gear;
My servants all for life did flee,
And left me in extremitie.

impounded; property

I sew'd his sheet, making my mane;
I watch'd the corpse, myself alane;
I watch'd his body, night and day;
No living creature came that way.

I took his body on my back,
And whiles I gaed, and whiles I sat;
I digg'd a grave, and laid him in,
And happ'd him with the sod sae green.

sometimes

wrapped

But think na ye my heart was sair,
When I laid the moul' on his yellow hair;
O think na ye my heart was wae,
When I turn'd about, away to gae?

Nae living man I'll love again,
Since that my lovely knight is slain;
Wi' ae lock of his yellow hair
I'll chain my heart for evermair.

Fair Helen

I wish I were where Helen lies,
Night and day on me she cries;
O that I were where Helen lies,
   On fair Kirconnell Lee!

Curst be the heart that thought the thought,
And curst the hand that fired the shot,
When in my arms burd Helen dropt,
   And died to succour me!

maid

O think na ye my heart was sair,
When my love dropt down and spak nae mair!
There did she swoon wi' meikle care,
   On fair Kirconnell Lee.

As I went down the water side,
None but my foe to be my guide,
None but my foe to be my guide,
   On fair Kirconnell Lee;

I lighted down, my sword to draw,
I hacked him in pieces sma',
I hacked him in pieces sma',
   For her sake that died for me.

O Helen fair, beyond compare!
I'll make a garland of thy hair,
Shall bind my heart for evermair,
   Until the day I die.

O that I were where Helen lies!
Night and day on me she cries;
Out of my bed she bids me rise,
   Says, 'Haste and come to me!'

O Helen fair! O Helen chaste!
If I were with thee, I were blest,
Where thou lies low, and takes thy rest,
   On fair Kirconnell Lee.

I wish my grave were growing green,
A winding sheet drawn ower my een,
And I in Helen's arms lying,
   On fair Kirconnell Lee.

I wish I were where Helen lies!
Night and day on me she cries;
And I am weary of the skies,
   For her sake that died for me.

Hughie the Græme

Gude Lord Scroope's to the hunting gane,
    He has ridden o'er moss and muir;
And he has grippit Hughie the Græme,
    For stealing o' the Bishop's mare.

'Now, good Lord Scroope, this may not be!
    Here hangs a broad sword by my side;
And if that thou canst conquer me,
    The matter it may soon be tryed.'

'I ne'er was afraid of a traitor thief;
    Although thy name be Hughie the Græme,
I'll make thee repent thee of thy deeds,
    If God but grant me life and time.'

'Then do your worst now, good Lord Scroope,
    And deal your blows as hard as you can!
It shall be tried within an hour,
    Which of us two is the better man.'

But as they were dealing their blows so free,
    And both so bloody at the time,
Over the moss came ten yeomen so tall,
    All for to take brave Hughie the Græme.

Then they hae grippit Hughie the Græme,
    And brought him up through Carlisle town;
The lasses and lads stood on the walls,
thou shalt   Crying, 'Hughie the Græme, thou'se ne'er gae
        down!'

Then they hae chosen a jury of men,
    The best that were in Carlisle town;
And twelve of them cried out at once,
    'Hughie the Græme, thou must gae down!'

Then up bespak him gude Lord Hume,
    As he sat by the judge's knee, —
'Twenty white owsen, my gude lord,   oxen
    If you'll grant Hughie the Græme to me.'

'O no, O no, my gude Lord Hume!
    For sooth and sae it mauna be;
For, were there but three Græmes of the name,
    They suld be hanged a' for me.'

'Twas up and spake the gude Lady Hume,
    As she sate by the judge's knee, —
'A peck of white pennies, my gude lord judge,
    If you'll grant Hughie the Græme to me.'

'O no, O no, my gude Lady Hume!
    Forsooth and so it mustna be;
Were he but the one Græme of the name,
    He suld be hanged high for me.'

'If I be guilty,' said Hughie the Græme,
    'Of me my friends shall have small talk';
And he has louped fifteen feet and three,   leapt
    Though his hands they were tied behind his
        back.

He looked over his left shoulder,
    And for to see what he might see;

There was he aware of his auld father,
    Came tearing his hair most piteously.

'O hald your tongue, my father,' he says,
    'And see that ye dinna weep for me!
For they may ravish me o' my life,
    But they canna banish me fro' heaven hie.

'Fare ye weel, fair Maggie, my wife!
    The last time we came ower the muir,
'Twas thou bereft me of my life,
    And wi' the bishop thou play'd the whore.

'Here, Johnie Armstrang, take thou my sword,
    That is made o' the metal sae fine;
And when thou comest to the English side,
    Remember the death of Hughie the Græme.'

Johnie of Cocklesmuir

Johnie rose up in a May morning,
 Call'd for water to wash his hands;
And he has call'd for his gude gray hunds,
 That lay bund in iron bands, bands,
 That lay bund in iron bands.

'Ye'll busk, ye'll busk my noble dogs,   *dress*
 Ye'll busk and mak them boun,   *ready*
For I'm going to the Broadspear-hill,
 To ding the dun deer doun, doun,   *beat*
 To ding the dun deer doun.'

Whan Johnie's mither heard o' this,
 She til her son has gane; —
'Ye'll win your mither's benison,
 Gin ye wad stay at hame, hame,   *If*
 Gin ye wad stay at hame.

Your meat sall be of the very, very best,
 And your drink o' the finest wine;
And ye will win your mither's benison,
 Gin ye wad stay at hame, hame,
 Gin ye wad stay at hame.'

His mither's counsel he wad na tak,
 Nor wad he stay at hame;
But he's on to the Broadspear-hill,
 To ding the dun deer doun, doun,
 To ding the dun deer doun.

Johnie lookit east, and Johnie lookit west,
And a little below the sun;
And there he spied the dun deer sleeping,
Aneath a buss o' brume, brume,
Aneath a buss o' brume.

<small>bush of broom</small>

Johnie shot, and the dun deer lap,
And he's woundit him in the side;
And atween the water and the wud,
He laid the dun deer's pride, pride,
He laid the dun deer's pride.

<small>sprang</small>

They ate sae meikle o' the venison,
And drank sae meikle o' the blude,
That Johnie and his twa gray hunds,
Fell asleep in yonder wud, wud,
Fell asleep in yonder wud.

By there cam a silly auld man,
And a silly auld man was he;
And he's aff to the proud foresters,
To tell what he did see, see,
To tell what he did see.

'What news, what news, my silly auld man,
What news, come tell to me?'
'Na news, na news,' said the silly auld man,
'But what my een did see, see,
But what my een did see,

'As I cam in by yon greenwud,
And doun amang the scrogs,

<small>bushes</small>

The bonniest youth that e'er I saw,
    Lay sleeping atween twa dogs, dogs,
    Lay sleeping atween twa dogs.

'The sark that he had on his back,   shirt
    Was o' the Holland sma';
And the coat that he had on his back,
    Was laced wi' gowd fu' braw, braw,   fine
    Was laced wi' gowd fu' braw.'

Up bespak the first forester,
    The first forester of a' —
'An this be Johnie o' Cocklesmuir,
    It's time we were awa, awa,
    It's time we were awa.'

Up bespak the niest forester,   next
    The niest forester of a' —
'An this be Johnie Cocklesmuir,
    To him we winna draw, draw,
    To him we winna draw.'

The first shot that they did shoot,
    They woundit him on the thie;
Up bespak the uncle's son, —
    'The niest will gar him die, die,   make
    The niest will gar him die.'

'Stand stout, stand stout, my noble dogs,
    Stand stout and dinna flee;
Stand fast, stand fast, my gude gray hunds,
    And we will mak them die, die,
    And we will mak them die.'

He has killed six o' the proud foresters,
   And wounded the seventh sair;
He laid his leg out owre his steed,
   Says, 'I will kill na mair, mair,'
   Says, 'I will kill na mair.'

The Laird o' Logie

I will sing, if ye will hearken,
　If ye will hearken unto me;
The King has ta'en a poor prisoner,
　The wanton laird o' young Logie.

Young Logie's laid in Edinburgh chapel;
　Carmichael's the keeper o' the key;
And may Margaret's lamenting sair,　　maiden
　A' for the love of young Logie.

'Lament, lament na, may Margaret,
　And of your weeping let me be;
For ye maun to the King himsell,
　To seek the life of young Logie.'

May Margaret has kilted her green cleiding,
　And she has curl'd back her yellow hair —
'If I canna get young Logie's life,
　Fareweel to Scotland for evermair.'

When she came before the King,
　She knelit lowly on her knee —
'O what's the matter, may Margaret?
　And what needs a' this courtesie?'

'A boon, a boon, my noble liege,
　A boon, a boon, I beg o' thee!
And the first boon that I come to crave,
　Is to grant me the life of young Logie.'

'O na, O na, may Margaret,
  Forsooth, and so it manna be;
For a' the gowd o' fair Scotland
  Shall not save the life of young Logie.'

dressing
comb

But she has stown the King's redding kaim,
  Likewise the Queen her wedding knife,
And sent the tokens to Carmichael,
  To cause young Logie get his life.

She sent him a purse o' the red gowd,
  Another o' the white monie;
She sent him a pistol for each hand,
  And bade him shoot when he gat free.

gaol

When he came to the tolbooth stair,
  There he let his volley flee;
It made the King in his chamber start,
  E'en in the bed where he might be.

'Gae out, gae out, my merrymen a',
  And bid Carmichael come speak to me;
For I'll lay my life the pledge o' that,
  That yon's the shot o' young Logie.'

When Carmichael came before the King,
  He fell low down upon his knee;
The very first word that the King spake,
  Was – 'Where's the laird of young Logie?'

Carmichael turn'd him round about,
  (I wot the tear blinded his e'e),
'There came a token frae your grace,
  Has ta'en away the laird frae me.'

'Hast thou play'd me that, Carmichael?
  And hast thou play'd me that?' quoth he;
'The morn the justice court's to stand,
  And Logie's place ye maun supplie.'

Carmichael's awa' to Margaret's bower,
  Even as fast as he may drie –   manage
'O if young Logie be within,
  Tell him to come and speak with me!'

May Margaret turn'd her round about
  (I wot a loud laugh laughed she),
'The egg is chipp'd, the bird is flown,
  Ye'll see nae mair of young Logie.'

The tane is shipped at the pier of Leith,   The one
  The tother at the Queen's Ferrie:
And she's gotten a father to her bairn,
  The wanton laird of young Logie.

A Lyke-Wake Dirge

This ae nighte, this ae nighte,
    Every night and alle;
house-room   Fire and fleet,* and candle lighte,
    And Christe receive thy saule.

When thou from hence away are paste,
    Every night and alle;
To Whinny-muir thou comest at laste;
    And Christe receive thye saule.

If ever thou gavest hosen and shoon,
    Every night and alle;
Sit thee down, and put them on;
    And Christe receive thye saule.

If hosen and shoon thou ne'er gavest nane,
    Every night and alle;
gorse   The whinnes shall pricke thee to the bare bane;
    And Christe receive thy saule.

From Whinny-muir when thou mayst passe,
    Every night and alle;
To Brigg o' Dread thou comest at laste;
    And Christe receive thye saule.

From Brigg o' Dread when thou mayst passe,
    Every night and alle;

* Scott reads 'sleet'; the correct 'fleet' comes from British
Museum Lansdowne MS. 231. For the legal phrase 'fire and
flet' see the Oxford *New English Dictionary* under 'flet'.

To purgatory fire thou comest at laste;
   And Christe receive thye saule.

If ever thou gavest meat or drink,
   Every night and alle;
The fire shall never make thee shrinke;
   And Christe receive thye saule.

If meate or drinke thou never gavest nane,
   Every night and alle;
The fire will burn thee to the bare bane;
   And Christe receive thye saule.

This ae nighte, this ae nighte,
   Every night and alle;
Fire and fleet, and candle lighte,
   And Christe receive thye saule.

The Dowie Dens of Yarrow

Late at e'en, drinking the wine,
    And ere they paid the lawing,
They set a combat them between,
    To fight it in the dawing.

'O stay at hame, my noble lord,
    O stay at hame, my marrow!
My cruel brother will you betray
    On the dowie houms of Yarrow.'

'O fare ye weel, my ladye gaye!
    O fare ye weel, my Sarah!
For I maun gae, though I ne'er return
    Frae the dowie banks o' Yarrow.'

She kiss'd his cheek, she kaim'd his hair,
    As oft she had done before, O;
She belted him with his noble brand,
    And he's away to Yarrow.

As he gaed up the Tennies bank,
    I wot he gaed wi' sorrow,
Till, down in a den, he spied nine arm'd men,
    On the dowie houms of Yarrow.

'O come ye here to part your land,
    The bonnie forest thorough?
Or come ye here to wield your brand,
    On the dowie houms of Yarrow?'

'I come not here to part my land,
  And neither to beg nor borrow;
I come to wield my noble brand,
  On the bonnie banks of Yarrow.'

'If I see all, ye're nine to ane;
  And that's an unequal marrow;   match
Yet will I fight, while lasts my brand,
  On the bonnie banks of Yarrow.'

Four has he hurt, and five has slain,
  On the bloody braes of Yarrow,
Till that stubborn knight came him behind,
  And ran his bodie thorough.

'Gae hame, gae hame, good-brother John,
  And tell your sister Sarah,
To come and lift her leafu' lord;   lawful
  He's sleepin sound on Yarrow.' –

'Yestreen I dream'd a dolefu' dream;
  I fear there will be sorrow!
I dream'd, I pu'd the heather green,
  Wi' my true love, on Yarrow.

'O gentle wind, that bloweth south,
  From where my love repaireth,
Convey a kiss from his dear mouth,
  And tell me how he fareth!

'But in the glen strive armed men;
  They've wrought me dole and sorrow;

They've slain – the comeliest knight they've
    slain –
  He bleeding lies on Yarrow.'

As she sped down yon high high hill,
  She gaed wi' dole and sorrow,
And in the den spied ten slain men,
  On the dowie banks of Yarrow.

She kiss'd his cheek, she kaim'd his hair,
  She search'd his wounds all thorough,
She kiss'd them, till her lips grew red,
  On the dowie houms of Yarrow.

'Now, haud your tongue, my daughter dear!
  For a' this breeds but sorrow;
I'll wed ye to a better lord,
  Than him ye lost on Yarrow.'

'O haud your tongue, my father dear,
  Ye mind me but of sorrow;
A fairer rose did never bloom
  Than now lies cropp'd on Yarrow.'

The Gay Goss-Hawk

'O waly, waly, my gay goss hawk,   *woe*
    Gin your feathering be sheen!'   *If; bright*
'And waly, waly, my master dear,
    Gin ye look pale and lean!

'O have ye tint, at tournament,   *lost*
    Your sword, or yet your spear?
Or mourn ye for the southern lass,
    Whom you may not win near?'   *reach*

'I have not tint, at tournament,
    My sword, nor yet my spear;
But sair I mourn for my true love,
    Wi' mony a bitter tear.

'But weel's me on ye, my gay goss-hawk, *I am for-*
    Ye can baith speak and flee;   *tunate in*
Ye sall carry a letter to my love,
    Bring an answer back to me.'

'But how sall I your true love find,
    Or how suld I her know?
I bear a tongue ne'er wi' her spake,
    An eye that ne'er her saw.'

'O weel sall ye my true love ken,
    Sae sune as ye her see;
For, of a' the flowers of fair England,
    The fairest flower is she.

'The red, that's on my true love's cheik,
    Is like blood-drops on the snaw;
The white, that is on her breast bare,
    Like the down o' the white sea-maw.

-gull

'And even at my love's bour door
    There grows a flowering birk;

birch

And ye maun sit and sing thereon
    As she gangs to the kirk.

'And four-and-twenty fair ladyes
    Will to the mass repair;
But weel may ye my ladye ken,
    The fairest ladye there.'

Lord William has written a love letter,
    Put it under his pinion gray;
And he is awa' to Southern land
    As fast as wings can gae.

And even at that ladye's bour
    There grew a flowering birk;
And he sat down and sung thereon
    As she gaed to the kirk.

And weel he kent that ladye fair
    Amang her maidens free;
For the flower, that springs in May morning,
    Was not sae sweet as she.

He lighted at the ladye's yate,
    And sat him on a pin;

piece of
wood

And sang fu' sweet the notes o' love,

quiet

    Till a' was cosh within.

And first he sang a low low note,
   And syne he sang a clear;   *next*
And aye the o'erword o' the sang   *burden*
   Was – 'Your love can no win here.'

'Feast on, feast on, my maidens a',
   The wine flows you amang,
While I gang to my shot-window,   *window*
   And hear yon bonny bird's sang.   *opening on*
                                    hinges

'Sing on, sing on, my bonny bird,
   The sang ye sung yestreen;
For weel I ken, by your sweet singing,
   Ye are frae my true love sen.'

O first he sang a merry sang,
   And syne he sang a grave;
And syne he peck'd his feathers gray,
   To her the letter gave.

'Have there a letter from Lord William;
   He says he's sent ye three;
He canna wait your love langer,
   But for your sake he'll die.'

'Gae bid him bake his bridal bread,
   And brew his bridal ale;
And I sall meet him at Mary's kirk,
   Lang, lang ere it be stale.'

The lady's gane to her chamber,
   And a moanfu' woman was she;
As gin she had ta'en a sudden brash,   *if; sickness*
   And were about to die.

'A boon, a boon, my father deir,
    A boon I beg of thee!'
haughty   'Ask not that paughty Scottish lord,
    For him you ne'er shall see.

'But, for your honest asking else,
    Weel granted it shall be.'
'Then, gin I die in Southern land,
cause   In Scotland gar bury me.

'And the first kirk that ye come to,
Ye shall   Ye's gar the mass be sung;
And the next kirk that ye come to,
    Ye's gar the bells be rung.

'And when ye come to St Mary's kirk,
    Ye's tarry there till night.'
And so her father pledged his word,
    And so his promise plight.

com-
modious   She has ta'en her to her bigly bour
    As fast as she could fare;
And she has drank a sleepy draught,
    That she had mix'd wi' care.

And pale, pale grew her rosy cheek,
complexion   That was sae bright of blee,
And she seemed to be as surely dead
    As any one could be.

-mother   Then spak her cruel step-minnie,
    'Tak ye the burning lead,
And drap a drap on her bosome,
    To try if she be dead.'

They took a drap o' boiling lead,
   They drapp'd it on her breast;
'Alas! alas!' her father cried,
   'She's dead without the priest.'

She neither chatter'd with her teeth,
   Nor shiver'd with her chin;
'Alas! alas!' her father cried,
   'There is nae breath within.'

Then up arose her seven brethren,
   And hew'd to her a bier;
They hew'd it frae the solid aik,
   Laid it o'er wi' silver clear.

Then up and gat her seven sisters,
   And sewed to her a kell;   cap
And every steek that they put in   stitch
   Sewed to a siller bell.

The first Scots kirk that they cam to,
   They garr'd the bells be rung;
The next Scots kirk that they cam to,
   They garr'd the mass be sung.

But when they cam to St Mary's kirk,
   There stude spearmen all on a raw;
And up and started Lord William,
   The chieftane amang them a'.

'Set down, set down the bier,' he said;
   'Let me look her upon:'

But as soon as Lord William touch'd her
    hand,
   Her colour began to come.

She brighten'd like the lily flower,
   Till her pale colour was gone;
With rosy cheik, and ruby lip,
   She smiled her love upon.

'A morsel of your bread, my lord,
   And one glass of your wine:
For I hae fasted these three lang days,
   All for your sake and mine.

'Gae hame, gae hame, my seven bauld
    brothers!
   Gae hame and blaw your horn!
I trow ye wad hae gi'en me the skaith,
   But I've gi'en you the scorn.

harm

'Commend me to my grey father,
   That wish'd my saul gude rest;
But wae be to my cruel step-dame,
   Gar'd burn me on the breast.'

'Ah! woe to you, you light woman!
   An ill death may you die!
For we left father and sisters at hame
   Breaking their hearts for thee.'

And kindly to him she did say,
   'It is time, true love, you were awa.'

But he lay still, and sleeped sound,
   Albeit the sun began to sheen;
She looked atween her and the wa',
   And dull and drowsie were his een.

Then in and came her father dear,
   Said – 'Let a' your mourning be:
I'll carry the dead corpse to the clay,
   And I'll come back and comfort thee.'

'Comfort weel your seven sons,
   For comforted will I never be:
I ween 'twas neither knave nor loon   low-born
   Was in the bower last night wi' me.' *

The clinking bell gaed through the town,
   To carry the dead corse to the clay;
And Clerk Saunders stood at may Margaret's
      window,
   I wot, an hour before the day.

'Are ye sleeping, Margaret?' he says,
   'Or are ye waking presentlie?
Give me my faith and troth again,
   I wot, true love, I gied to thee.'

'Your faith and troth ye sall never get,
   Nor our true love sall never twin,   part
Until ye come within my bower,
   And kiss me cheik and chin.'

* The rest is a version of *Sweet William's Ghost* (Child No. 77).

'My mouth it is full cold, Margaret,
　　It has the smell, now, of the ground;
And if I kiss thy comely mouth,
　　Thy days of life will not be lang.

'O, cocks are crowing a merry midnight,
　　I wot the wild fowls are boding day;
Give me my faith and troth again,
　　And let me fare me on my way.'

'Thy faith and troth thou sall na get,
　　And our true love sall never twin,
Until ye tell what comes of women,
travail　　I wot, who die in strong traivelling?'

'Their beds are made in the heavens high,
　　Down at the foot of our good Lord's knee,
Weel set about wi' gillyflowers;
　　I wot sweet company for to see.

'O cocks are crowing a merry midnight,
　　I wot the wild fowl are boding day;
The psalms of heaven will soon be sung,
　　And I, ere now, will be miss'd away.'

Then she has ta'en a crystal wand,
struck　　And she has stroken* her troth thereon;
window　She has given it him out at the shot-window,
opening on
hinges　　Wi' mony a sad sigh, and heavy groan.

'I thank ye, Marg'ret; I thank ye, Marg'ret;
　　And aye I thank ye heartilie;
Gin ever the dead come for the quick,
　　Be sure, Marg'ret, I'll come for thee.'

* In Herd's MS. 'straked', i.e. 'stroked'.

Its hosen and shoon, and gown alone,
　　She climb'd the wall, and follow'd him,
Until she came to the green forest,
　　And there she lost the sight o' him.

'Is there ony room at your head, Saunders?
　　Is there ony room at your feet?
Or ony room at your side, Saunders,
　　Where fain, fain, I wad sleep?'

'There's nae room at my head, Marg'ret,
　　There's nae room at my feet;
My bed it is full lowly now:
　　Amang the hungry worms I sleep.

'Cauld mould is my covering now,
　　But and my winding-sheet;　　　　　　And also
The dew it falls nae sooner down,
　　Than my resting place is weet.

'But plait a wand o' bonnie birk,
　　And lay it on my breast;
And shed a tear upon my grave,
　　And wish my saul gude rest.

'And fair Marg'ret, and rare Marg'ret,
　　And Marg'ret o' veritie,
Gin e'er ye love another man,
　　Ne'er love him as ye did me.'

Then up and crew the milk-white cock,
　　And up and crew the grey;
Her lover vanish'd in the air,
　　And she gaed weeping away.

'O where have you been, my long, long love,
    This long seven years and mair?'
'O I'm come to seek my former vows
    Ye granted me before.'

'O hold your tongue of your former vows,
    For they will breed sad strife;
O hold your tongue of your former vows,
    For I am become a wife.'

He turn'd him right and round about,
    And the tear blinded his e'e;
'I wad never hae trodden on Irish ground
    If it had not been for thee.

'I might hae had a king's daughter,
    Far, far beyond the sea;
I might have had a king's daughter,
    Had it not been for love o' thee.'

'If ye might have had a king's daughter,
    Yer sel ye had to blame;
Ye might have taken the king's daughter,
    For ye kend that I was nane.'

'O faulse are the vows of womankind,
    But fair is their faulse bodie;
I never wad hae trodden on Irish ground,
    Had it not been for love o' thee.'

'If I was to leave my husband dear,
   And my two babes also,
O what have you to take me to,
   If with you I should go?'

'I hae seven ships upon the sea,
   The eighth brought me to land;
With four-and-twenty bold mariners,
   And music on every hand.'

She has taken up her two little babes,
   Kiss'd them baith cheek and chin;
'O fair ye weel, my ain two babes,
   For I'll never see you again.'

She set her foot upon the ship,
   No mariners could she behold;
But the sails were o' the taffetie,
   And the masts o' the beaten gold.

She had not sail'd a league, a league,
   A league but barely three,
When dismal grew his countenance,
   And drumlie grew his e'e.   *sullen*

The masts that were like the beaten gold,
   Bent not on the heaving seas;
But the sails, that were o' the taffetie,
   Fill'd not in the east land breeze.

They had not sailed a league, a league,
   A league but barely three,
Until she espied his cloven foot,
   And she wept right bitterlie.

'O hold your tongue of your weeping,' says he,
   'Of your weeping now let me be;
I will show you how the lilies grow
   On the banks of Italy.'

'O what hills are yon, yon pleasant hills,
   That the sun shines sweetly on?'
'O yon are the hills of heaven,' he said,
go   'Where you will never win.'

what sort 'O whaten a mountain is yon,' she said,
of   'All so dreary wi' frost and snow?'
'O yon is the mountain of hell,' he cried,
   'Where you and I will go.'

And aye when she turn'd her round about,
   Aye taller he seem'd for to be;
Until that the tops o' that gallant ship
   Nae taller were than he.

The clouds grew dark, and the wind grew loud,
lightning And the levin fill'd her e'e;
And waesome wail'd the snow-white sprites
roaring   Upon the gurlie sea.

He strack the tap-mast wi' his hand,
   The fore-mast wi' his knee;
And he brake that gallant ship in twain,
   And sank her in the sea.

Fair Annie of Lochroyan

'O wha will shoe my fair foot,
  And wha will glove my han'?
And wha will lace my middle gimp   slender
  Wi' a new-made London ban'?

'Or wha will kemb my yellow hair
  Wi' a new-made silver kemb?
Or wha'll be father to my young bairn,
  Till love Gregor come hame?'

'Your father'll shoe your fair foot,
  Your mother glove your han';
Your sister lace your middle jimp
  Wi' a new-made London ban';

'Your brethren will kemb your yellow hair
  Wi' a new-made silver kemb;
And the King o' Heaven will father your
      bairn,
  Till love Gregor come hame.'

'O gin I had a bonny ship,   if
  And men to sail wi' me,
It's I wad gang to my true love,
  Sin he winna come to me!'

Her father's gien her a bonny ship,
  And sent her to the stran';
She's taen her young son in her arms,
  And turn'd her back to the lan'.

She hadna been o' the sea sailin'
    About a month or more,
Till landed has she her bonny ship
    Near her true-love's door.

The nicht was dark, and the wind blew cald,
    And her love was fast asleep,
And the bairn that was in her twa arms

cry

    Fu' sair began to greet.

Lang stood she at her true love's door,

rattled

    And lang tirl'd at the pin;
At length up gat his fause mother,
    Says, 'Wha's that wad be in?'

'O, it is Annie of Lochroyan,
    Your love, come o'er the sea,

And also

But and your young son in her arms;
    So open the door to me.'

'Awa, awa, ye ill woman,
    You're nae come here for gude;
You're but a witch, or a vile warlock,
    Or mermaid o' the flude.'

'I'm nae a witch or vile warlock,
    Or mermaiden,' said she; —
'I'm but your Annie of Lochroyan; —
    O open the door to me!'

'O gin ye be Annie of Lochroyan,
    As I trust not ye be,
What taiken can ye gie that e'er
    I kept your companie?'

'O dinna ye mind, love Gregor,' she says,
    'Whan we sat at the wine,
How we changed the napkins frae our necks,
    It's nae sae lang sinsyne?   *ago*

'And yours was gude, and gude enough;
    But nae sae gude as mine;
For yours was o' the cambrick clear,
    But mine o' the silk sae fine.

'And dinna ye mind, love Gregor,' she says,
    'As we twa sat at dine,
How we chang'd the rings frae our fingers,
    And I can shew thee thine:

'And yours was gude, and gude enough,
    Yet nae sae gude as mine;
For yours was o' the gude red gold,
    But mine o' the diamonds fine.

'Sae open the door, now, love Gregor,
    And open it wi' speed;
Or your young son, that is in my arms,
    For cald will soon be dead.'

'Awa, awa, ye ill woman;
    Gae frae my door for shame,
For I hae gotten anither fair love,
    Sae ye may hie you hame.'

'O hae ye gotten anither fair love,
    For a' the oaths ye sware?
Then fare ye weel, now, fause Gregor;
    For me ye's never see mair!'   *ye shall*

slowly

O, hooly hooly gaed she back,
  As the day began to peep;
She set her foot on good ship board,
  And sair sair did she weep.

'Tak down, tak down the mast o' goud;
wood   Set up the mast o' tree;
becomes Ill sets it a forsaken lady
  To sail sae gallantlie.

'Tak down, tak down the sails o' silk;
  Set up the sails o' skin;
Ill sets the outside to be gay,
  Whan there's sic grief within!'

Love Gregor started frae his sleep,
  And to his mother did say,
'I dreamt a dream this night, mither,
  That maks my heart richt wae;

'I dreamt that Annie of Lochroyan,
  The flower o' a' her kin,
Was standin' mournin' at my door,
  But nane wad lat her in.'

'O there was a woman stood at the door,
  Wi' a bairn intill her arms;
But I wadna let her within the bower,
  For fear she had done you harm.'

O quickly, quickly raise he up,
  And fast ran to the strand;
And there he saw her, fair Annie,
  Was sailing frae the land.

And 'heigh, Annie,' and 'how, Annie!
   O, Annie, winna ye bide?'
But ay the louder that he cried 'Annie,'
   The higher rair'd the tide.

And 'heigh, Annie!' and 'how, Annie!
   O, Annie, speak to me!'
But ay the louder that he cried 'Annie,'
   The louder rair'd the sea.

The wind grew loud, and the sea grew rough,
   And the ship was rent in twain;
And soon he saw her, fair Annie,
   Come floating o'er the main.

He saw his young son in her arms,
   Baith toss'd aboon the tide;
He wrang his hands, and fast he ran,
   And plunged in the sea sae wide.

He catch'd her by the yellow hair,
   And drew her to the strand;
But cald and stiff was every limb,
   Before he reach'd the land.

O first he kist her cherry cheek,
   And syne he kist her chin,   next
And sair he kist her ruby lips;
   But there was nae breath within.

O he has mourn'd o'er fair Annie,
   Till the sun was ganging down;
Syne wi' a sich his heart it brast,   sigh; burst
   And his saul to heaven has flown.

Kempion

'Cum heir, cum heir, ye freely feed, *[of noble birth]*
  And lay your head low on my knee;
The heaviest weird I will you read, *[fate]*
  That ever was read to gay ladye.

'O meikle dolour sall ye dree, *[bear]*
  And aye the salt seas o'er ye'se swim; *[ye shall]*
And far mair dolour sall ye dree
  On Estmere crags, when ye them climb.

'I weird ye to a fiery beast, *[doom]*
  And relieved sall ye never be,
Till Kempion, the kingis son,
  Cum to the crag, and thrice kiss thee.'

O meikle dolour did she dree,
  And aye the salt seas o'er she swam;
And far mair dolour did she dree
  On Estmere crags, e'er she them clamb.

And aye she cried for Kempion,
  Gin he would but come to her hand: *[If]*
Now word has gane to Kempion,
  That sicken a beast was in his land. *[such]*

'Now, by my sooth,' said Kempion,
  'This fiery beast I'll gang and see.'
'And by my sooth,' said Segramour,
  'My ae brother, I'll gang wi' thee.'

Then bigged hae they a bonny boat,   built
 And they hae set her to the sea;
But a mile before they reach'd the shore,
 Around them she gar'd the red fire flee. made

'O Segramour, keep the boat afloat,
 And let her na the land o'er near;
For this wicked beast will sure gae mad,
 And set fire to a' the land and mair.'

Syne has he bent an arblast bow,   Then;
 And aim'd an arrow at her head;   crossbow
And swore if she didna quit the land,
 Wi' that same shaft to shoot her dead.

'O out of my stythe I winna rise   place
 (And it is not for the awe o' thee),
Till Kempion, the kingis son,
 Cum to the crag, and thrice kiss me.'

He has louted him o'er the dizzy crag,   bent
 And gi'en the monster kisses ane;
Awa she gaed, and again she cam,
 The fieryest beast that ever was seen.

'O out o' my stythe I winna rise
 (And not for a' thy bow nor thee),
Till Kempion, the kingis son,
 Cum to the crag, and thrice kiss me.'

He's louted him o'er the Estmere crags,
 And he has gi'en her kisses twa:
Awa she gaed, and again she cam,
 The fieryest beast that ever you saw.

'O out of my den I winna rise,
    Nor flee it for the fear o' thee,
'Till Kempion, that courteous knight,
    Cum to the crag, and thrice kiss me.'

He's louted him o'er the lofty crag,
    And he has gi'en her kisses three:
Awa' she gaed, and again she cam,
    The loveliest ladye e'er could be.

'And by my sooth,' says Kempion,
    'My ain true love (for this is she),
They surely had a heart o' stane,
    Could put thee to such misery.

'O was it warwolf in the wood?
    Or was it mermaid in the sea?
Or was it man, or vile woman,
    My ain true love, that mishaped thee?'

'It wasna warwolf in the wood,
    Nor was it mermaid in the sea;
But it was my wicked step-mother,
    And wae and weary may she be!'

'O a heavier weird shall light her on,
    Than ever fell on vile woman;
Her hair shall grow rough, and her teeth grow
        lang,
    And on her four feet shall she gang.

'None shall take pity her upon;
    In Wormeswood she aye shall won;

live

202

And relieved shall she never be,
    Till St Mungo come over the sea.'
And, sighing, said that weary wight,
    'I doubt that day I'll never see!'

Lord Thomas and Fair Annie

'It's narrow, narrow, make your bed,
    And learn to lie your lane;
For I'm gaun o'er the sea, Fair Annie,
    A braw bride to bring hame.

property

Wi' her I will get gowd and gear;
    Wi' you I ne'er got nane.

'But wha will bake my bridal bread,
    Or brew my bridal ale?
And wha will welcome my brisk bride,
    That I bring o'er the dale?'

'It's I will bake your bridal bread,
    And brew your bridal ale;
And I will welcome your brisk bride,
    That you bring o'er the dale.'

'But she that welcomes my brisk bride,
    Maun gang like maiden fair;

neat

She maun lace on her robe sae jimp,
    And braid her yellow hair.'

'But how can I gang maiden-like,
    When maiden I am nane?
Have I not born seven sons to thee,
    And am with child again?'

She's ta'en her young son in her arms,
    Another in her hand;

And she's up to the highest tower,
    To see him come to land.

'Come up, come up, my eldest son,
    And look o'er yon sea-strand,
And see your father's new-come bride,
    Before she come to land.'

'Come down, come down, my mother dear!
    Come frae the castle-wa'!
I fear, if langer ye stand there,
    Ye'll let yoursell down fa'.'

And she gaed down, and farther down,
    Her love's ship for to see;
And the top-mast and the main-mast
    Shone like the silver free.

And she's gane down, and farther down,
    The bride's ship to behold;
And the top-mast and the main-mast
    They shone just like the gold.

She's ta'en her seven sons in her hand;
    I wot she didna fail!
She met Lord Thomas and his bride,
    As they came o'er the dale.

'You're welcome to your house, Lord Thomas;
    You're welcome to your land;
You're welcome, with your fair ladye,
    That you lead by the hand.

'You're welcome to your ha's, ladye;
  You're welcome to your bowers;
You're welcome to your hame, ladye,
  For a' that's here is yours.'

'I thank thee, Annie; I thank thee, Annie;
  Sae dearly as I thank thee;
You're the likest to my sister, Annie,
  That ever I did see.

'There came a knight out o'er the sea,
  And steal'd my sister away;
devil run The shame scoup in his company,
  And land where'er he gae!'

She hang ae napkin at the door,
  Another in the ha';
And a' to wipe the trickling tears,
  Sae fast as they did fa'.

And aye she served the lang tables,
  With white bread and with wine;
And aye she drank the wan water,
keep To had her colour fine.

And aye she served the lang tables,
  With white bread and with brown;
And aye she turned her round about,
  Sae fast the tears fell down.

And he's ta'en down the silk napkin,
  Hung on a silver pin;
And aye he wipes the tear trickling
  Adown her cheik and chin.

And aye he turn'd him round about,
  And smiled amang his men,
Says — 'Like ye best the old ladye,
  Or her that's new come hame?'

When bells were rung, and mass was sung,
  And a' men bound to bed,
Lord Thomas and his new-come bride,
  To their chamber they were gaed.

Annie made her bed a little forbye,   near by
  To hear what they might say;
'And ever alas!' fair Annie cried,
  'That I should see this day!

'Gin my seven sons were seven young rats,
  Running on the castle-wa',
And I were a gray cat mysell,
  I soon would worry them a'.

'Gin my seven sons were seven young hares,
  Running o'er yon lilly lee,   lovely
And I were a grew hound mysell,   greyhound
  Soon worried they a' should be.'

And wae and sad fair Annie sat,
  And drearie was her sang;
And ever, as she sobb'd and grat,
  'Wae to the man that did the wrang!'

'My gown is on,' said the new-come bride,
  'My shoes are on my feet,
And I will to fair Annie's chamber,
  And see what gars her greet. —   makes;
                                                    weep

'What ails ye, what ails ye, Fair Annie,
    That ye make sic a moan?
Has your wine barrels cast the girds,
    Or is your white bread gone?

hoops

'O wha was't was your father, Annie,
    Or wha was't was your mother?
And had ye ony sister, Annie,
    Or had ye ony brother?'

'The Earl of Wemyss was my father,
    The Countess of Wemyss my mother:
And a' the folk about the house,
    To me were sister and brother.'

'If the Earl of Wemyss was your father,
    I wot sae was he mine;
And it shall not be for lack o' gowd,
lose   That ye your love sall tyne.

'For I have seven ships o' mine ain,
    A' loaded to the brim;
And I will gie them a' to thee,
    Wi' four to thine eldest son.
But thanks to a' the powers in heaven,
    That I gae maiden hame!'

The Wife of Usher's Well

There lived a wife at Usher's Well,
    And a wealthy wife was she;
She had three stout and stalwart sons,
    And sent them o'er the sea.

They hadna been a week from her,
    A week but barely ane,
When word came to the carline wife,   old woman
    That her three sons were gane.

They hadna been a week from her,
    A week but barely three,
When word came to the carline wife,
    That her sons she'd never see.

'I wish the wind may never cease,
    Nor fishes* in the flood,
Till my three sons come hame to me,
    In earthly flesh and blood!'

It fell about the Martinmas,
    When nights are lang and mirk,   murky
The carline wife's three sons came hame,
    And their hats were o' the birk.   birch

It neither grew in syke nor ditch,   marshy
    Nor yet in ony sheugh;   stream / ravine
But at the gates o' Paradise,
    That birk grew fair eneugh.

*

* 'Fashes' meaning 'troubles' is the conjecture of Lockhart,
in the 1833 edition of the *Minstrelsy*.

'Blow up the fire, my maidens!
  Bring water from the well!
For a' my house shall feast this night,
  Since my three sons are well.'

And she has made to them a bed,
  She's made it large and wide;
And she's ta'en her mantle her about,
  Sat down at the bed-side.

*

Up then crew the red red cock,
  And up and crew the gray;
The eldest to the youngest said,
  ''Tis time we were away.'

The cock he hadna craw'd but once,
  And clapp'd his wings at a',
Whan the youngest to the eldest said,
  'Brother, we must awa.

'The cock doth craw, the day doth daw,
fretting   The channerin' worm doth chide;
If   Gin we be mist out o' our place,
suffer   A sair pain we maun bide.

'Fare ye weel, my mother dear!
  Fareweel to barn and byre!
And fare ye weel, the bonny lass,
  That kindles my mother's fire.'

Cospatrick

Cospatrick has sent o'er the faem;
Cospatrick brought his ladye hame;
And fourscore ships have come her wi',
The ladye by the grene-wood tree.

There were twal' and twal' wi' baken bread,
And twal' and twal' wi' gowd sae reid,
And twal' and twal' wi' bouted flour,   sifted
And twal' and twal' wi' the paramour.

Sweet Willy was a widow's son,
And at her stirrup he did run;
And she was clad in the finest pall,   cloth
But aye she let the tears down fall.

'O is your saddle set awrye?
Or rides your steed for you owre high?
Or are you mourning, in your tide,
That you suld be Cospatrick's bride?'

'I am not mourning, at this tide,
That I suld be Cospatrick's bride;
But I am sorrowing in my mood,
That I suld leave my mother good.

'But, gentle boy, come tell to me,
What is the custom of thy countrie?'
'The custom thereof, my dame,' he says,
'Will ill a gentle lady please.

'Seven king's daughters has our lord wedded,
And seven king's daughters has our lord bedded;
But he's cutted their breasts frae their breast-
    bane,
And sent them mourning hame again.

'Yet, gin you're sure that you're a maid,
Ye may gae safely to his bed;
But gif o' that ye be na sure,
Then hire some damsell o' your bour.'

The ladye's called her bour maiden,
That waiting was into her train;
'Five thousand merks I'll gie to thee,
To sleep this night with my lord for me.'

When bells were rung, and mass was sayne,
And a' men unto bed were gane,
Cospatrick and the bonny maid,
Into ae chamber they were laid.

'Now, speak to me, blankets, and speak to me,
    bed,
And speak, thou sheet, enchanted web;
And speak up, my bonny brown sword, that
    winna lie,
Is this a true maiden that lies by me?'

'It is not a maid that you hae wedded,
But it is a maid that you hae bedded;
true   It is a leal maiden that lies by thee,
But not the maiden that it should be.'

O wrathfully he left the bed,
And wrathfully his claes on did;
And he has ta'en him through the ha',
And on his mother he did ca'.

'I am the most unhappy man,
That ever was in Christen land!
I courted a maiden, meik and mild,
And I hae gotten naething but a woman
     wi' child.'

'O stay, my son, into this ha',
And sport ye wi' your merrymen a';
And I will to the secret bour,
To see how it fares wi' your paramour.'

The carline she was stark and sture,   strong;
She aff the hinges dang the dure;   stout
'O is your bairn to laird or loun,   peasant
Or is it to your father's groom?'

'O hear me, mother, on my knee,
Till my sad story I tell to thee:
O we were sisters, sisters seven,
We were the fairest under heaven.

'It fell on a summer's afternoon,
When a' our toilsome task was done,
We cast the kevils us amang,   lots
To see which suld to the grene-wood gang.

'O hon! alas, for I was youngest,
And aye my wierd it was the hardest!   fate

213

The kevil it on me did fa',
Whilk was the cause of a' my woe.

'For to the grene-wood I maun gae,
sloe   To pu' the red rose and the slae;
To pu' the red rose and the thyme,
To deck my mother's bour and mine.

'I hadna pu'd a flower but ane,
kind   When by there came a gallant hende,
cut; low   Wi' high coll'd hose and laigh coll'd shoon,
And he seem'd to be sum kingis son.

'And be I a maid, or be I nae,
He kept me there till the close o' day;
And be I a maid, or be I nane,
He kept me there till the day was done.

'He gae me a lock o' his yellow hair,
And bade me keep it ever mair;
necklace   He gae me a carknet o' bonny beads,
And bade me keep it against my needs.

'He gae to me a gay gold ring,
And bade me keep it abune a' thing.'
'What did ye wi' the tokens rare,
That ye gat frae that gallant there?'

'O bring that coffer unto me,
And a' the tokens ye sall see.'
'Now stay, daughter, your bour within,
While I gae parley wi' my son.'

O she has ta'en her thro' the ha',
And on her son began to ca';
'What did ye wi' the bonny beads,
I bade ye keep against your needs?

'What did you wi' the gay gold ring,
I bade you keep abune a' thing?'
'I gae them to a ladye gay,
I met on grene-wood on a day.

'But I wad gie a' my halls and tours,
I had that ladye within my bours;
But I wad gie my very life,
I had that ladye to my wife.'

'Now keep, my son, your ha's and tours,
Ye have the bright burd in your bours;   girl
And keep, my son, your very life,
Ye have that ladye to your wife.'

Now, or a month was come and gane,
The ladye bare a bonny son;
And 'twas weel written on his breast-bane,
'Cospatrick is my father's name.'
O row my lady in satin and silk,   wrap
And wash my son in the morning milk.

The Twa Sisters

There was twa sisters liv'd in a bower,
    (Binnorie, O Binnorie!)
There came a knight to be their wooer,
    By the bonny mill-dams o' Binnorie.

He courted the eldest wi' glove and ring,
    (Binnorie, O Binnorie!)
But he loved the youngest aboon a' thing,
    By the bonny mill-dams o' Binnorie.

He courted the eldest wi' broach and knife,
    (Binnorie, O Binnorie!)
But he loved the youngest as his life,
    By the bonny mill-dams o' Binnorie.

The eldest she was vexed sair,
    (Binnorie, O Binnorie!)
And sair envied her sister fair,
    By the bonny mill-dams o' Binnorie.

Intill her bower she coudna rest,
    (Binnorie, O Binnorie!)
Wi' grief and spite she maistly brast,
    By the bonny mill-dams o' Binnorie.

almost burst [margin gloss]

Upon a morning fair and clear,
    (Binnorie, O Binnorie!)
She cried upon her sister dear,
    By the bonny mill-dams o' Binnorie.

'O sister, come to yon sea strand,
    (Binnorie, O Binnorie!)
And see our father's ships come to land,
    By the bonny mill-dams o' Binnorie.'

She's ta'en her by the milk-white hand,
    (Binnorie, O Binnorie!)
And led her down to yon sea strand,
    By the bonny mill-dams o' Binnorie.

The youngest stood upon a stane,
    (Binnorie, O Binnorie!)
The eldest came and threw her in,
    By the bonny mill-dams o' Binnorie.

She took her by the middle sma',
    (Binnorie, O Binnorie!)
And dashed her bonny back to the jaw,   water
    By the bonny mill-dams o' Binnorie.

'O sister, sister, tak my hand,
    (Binnorie, O Binnorie!)
And I'se mak ye heir to a' my land,   I shall
    By the bonny mill-dams o' Binnorie.

'O sister, sister, tak my middle,
    (Binnorie, O Binnorie!)
And ye's get my goud and my gouden girdle,
    By the bonny mill-dams o' Binnorie.

'O sister, sister, save my life,
    (Binnorie, O Binnorie!)
And I swear I'se never be nae man's wife,
    By the bonny mill-dams o' Binnorie.'

'Foul fa' the hand that I should tak,
    (Binnorie, O Binnorie!)
It twin'd me o' my wardles mak,
      By the bonny mill-dams o' Binnorie.

deprived; earthly mate

'Your cherry cheeks and yellow hair
    (Binnorie, O Binnorie!)
Gars me gang maiden for evermair,
      By the bonny mill-dams o' Binnorie.'

Makes

Sometimes she sank, sometimes she swam,
    (Binnorie, O Binnorie!)
Till she came to the mouth o' yon mill-dam
      By the bonny mill-dams o' Binnorie.

O out it came the miller's son,
    (Binnorie, O Binnorie!)
And saw the fair maid soummin in,
      By the bonny mill-dams o' Binnorie.

'O father, father, draw your dam,
    (Binnorie, O Binnorie!)
There's either a mermaid or a swan,
      By the bonny mill-dams o' Binnorie.'

*

You coudna see her yellow hair
    (Binnorie, O Binnorie!)
For goud and pearl that was sae rare,
      By the bonny mill-dams o' Binnorie.

You coudna see her middle sma'
    (Binnorie, O Binnorie!)
For gouden girdle that was sae braw,
      By the bonny mill-dams o' Binnorie.

You coudna see her fingers white
  (Binnorie, O Binnorie!)
For gouden rings that were sae gryte,   great
  By the bonny mill-dams o' Binnorie.

And by there came a harper fine,
  (Binnorie, O Binnorie!)
That harped to the king at dine,
  By the bonny mill-dams o' Binnorie.

When he did look that lady upon,
  (Binnorie, O Binnorie!)
He sigh'd and made a heavy moan,
  By the bonny mill-dams o' Binnorie.

He's ta'en three locks o' her yellow hair,
  (Binnorie, O Binnorie!)
And wi' them strung his harp sae fair,
  By the bonny mill-dams o' Binnorie.

The first tune it did play and sing,
  (Binnorie, O Binnorie!)
Was, 'Fareweel to my father the king,
  By the bonny mill-dams o' Binnorie.'

The nexten tune that it play'd seen   then
  (Binnorie, O Binnorie!)
Was, 'Fareweel to my mither the queen,
  By the bonny mill-dams o' Binnorie.'

The thirden tune that it play'd then,
  (Binnorie, O Binnorie!)
Was, 'Wae to my sister, fair Ellen,
  By the bonny mill-dams o' Binnorie!'

Marie Hamilton

Word's gane to the kitchen,
    And word's gane to the ha',
That Marie Hamilton gangs wi' bairn,
    To the hichest Stewart of a'.

He's courted her in the kitchen,
    He's courted her in the ha',
low He's courted her in the laigh cellar,
    And that was warst of a'!

She's tyed it in her apron,
    And she's thrown it in the sea,
Says, 'Sink ye, swim ye, bonny wee babe,
    You'l ne'er get mair o' me.'

Down then cam the auld Queen,
    Goud tassels tying her hair —
'O, Marie, where's the bonny wee babe,
cry That I heard greet sae sair?'

'There was never a babe intill my room,
    As little designs to be;
It was but a touch o' my sair side,
    Come o'er my fair bodie.'

'O, Marie, put on your robes o' black,
    Or else your robes o' brown,
For ye maun gang wi' me the night,
    To see fair Edinbro' town.'

'I winna put on my robes o' black,
   Nor yet my robes o' brown,
But I'll put on my robes o' white,
   To shine through Edinbro' town.'

When she gaed up the Cannogate,
   She laugh'd loud laughters three;
But whan she cam down the Cannogate,
   The tear blinded her e'e.

When she gaed up the Parliament stair,
   The heel cam aff her shee,
And lang or she cam down again,
   She was condemn'd to dee.

When she cam down the Cannogate,
   The Cannogate sae free,
Mony a ladie look'd o'er her window,
   Weeping for this ladie.

'Ye need nae weep for me,' she says,
   'Ye need nae weep for me,
For had I not slain mine own sweet babe,
   This death I wadna dee.

'Bring me a bottle of wine,' she says,
   'The best that e'er ye hae,
That I may drink to my weil wishers,
   And they may drink to me.

'Here's a health to the jolly sailors,
   That sail upon the main,
Let them never let on to my father and mother, tell
   But what I'm coming hame.

'Here's a health to the jolly sailors,
   That sail upon the sea;
Let them never let on to my father and mothe
   That I cam here to dee.

'Oh, little did my mother think,
   The day she cradled me,
What lands I was to travel through,
   What death I was to dee.

'Oh, little did my father think,
   The day he held up me,
What lands I was to travel through,
   What death I was to dee.

'Last night I wash'd the Queen's feet,
   And gently laid her down;
And a' the thanks I've gotten the nicht,
   To be hang'd in Edinbro' town.

'Last nicht there was four Maries,
   The nicht there'l be but three;
There was Marie Seton, and Marie Beton,
   And Marie Carmichael, and me.'

Thomas the Rhymer

True Thomas lay on Huntlie bank;
  A ferlie he spied wi' his e'e;   *wonder*
And there he saw a ladye bright,
  Come riding down by the Eildon Tree.

Her shirt was o' the grass-green silk,
  Her mantle o' the velvet fyne;
At ilka tett of her horse's mane,   *every lock*
  Hung fifty siller bells and nine.

True Thomas, he pull'd aff his cap,
  And louted low down to his knee,   *beat*
'All hail, thou mighty Queen of Heav'n!
  For thy peer on earth I never did see.'

'O no, O no, Thomas,' she said;
  'That name does not belang to me;
I am but the Queen of fair Elfland,
  That am hither come to visit thee.

'Harp and carp, Thomas,' she said;   *recite (as a minstrel)*
  'Harp and carp along wi' me;
And if ye dare to kiss my lips,
  Sure of your bodie I will be.'

'Betide me weal, betide me woe,
  That weird shall never danton me.'   *fate; daunt*
Syne he has kiss'd her rosy lips,   *Next*
  All underneath the Eildon Tree.

'Now, ye maun go wi' me,' she said;
  'True Thomas, ye maun go wi' me;
And ye maun serve me seven years,
  Thro' weal or woe as may chance to be.'

She mounted on her milk-white steed;
  She's ta'en true Thomas up behind:
And aye, whene'er her bridle rung,
  The steed flew swifter than the wind.

O they rade on, and farther on;
  The steed gaed swifter than the wind;
Until they reach'd a desart wide,
  And living land was left behind.

'Light down, light down, now, true Thomas,
  And lean your head upon my knee:
Abide and rest a little space,
  And I will show you ferlies three.

'O see ye not yon narrow road,
  So thick beset with thorns and briers?
That is the path of righteousness,
  Though after it but few enquires.

'And see not ye that braid braid road,
  That lies across that lily leven?
That is the path of wickedness,
  Though some call it the road to heaven.

'And see not ye that bonny road,
  That winds about the fernie brae?
That is the road to fair Elfland,
  Where thou and I this night maun gae.

lovely (?)
lawn

224

'But, Thomas, ye maun hold your tongue,
    Whatever ye may hear or see;
For, if you speak word in Elflyn land,
    Ye'll ne'er get back to your ain countrie.'

O they rade on, and farther on,
    And they waded through rivers aboon the
        knee,
And they saw neither sun nor moon,
    But they heard the roaring of the sea.

It was mirk mirk night, and there was nae stern star
        light,
    And they waded through red blude to the
        knee;
For a' the blude, that's shed on earth,
    Rins through the springs o' that countrie.

Syne they came on to a garden green,
    And she pu'd an apple frae a tree –
'Take this for thy wages, true Thomas;
    It will give thee the tongue that can never
        lie.'

'My tongue is mine ain,' true Thomas said;
    'A gudely gift ye wad gie to me!
I neither dought to buy nor sell,   could
    At fair or tryst where I may be.

'I dought neither speak to prince or peer,
    Nor ask of grace from fair ladye.'
'Now hold thy peace!' the lady said,
    'For as I say, so must it be.'

smooth

He has gotten a coat of the even cloth,
  And a pair of shoes of velvet green;
And, till seven years were gane and past,
  True Thomas on earth was never seen.

O waly, waly, up the Bank,
  And waly, waly down the Brae,
And waly, waly yon Burn-Side,
  Where I and my Love wont to gae.
I lean'd my Back unto an Aik,
  I thought it was a trusty Tree,
But first it bow'd and syne it brak,   next
  Sae my true Love did lightly me.   slight

O waly, waly, but Love be bony,
  A little Time while it is new,
But when 'tis auld it waxeth cauld,
  And fades away like the Morning Dew.
O wherefore shou'd I busk my Head?   dress
  Or wherefore shou'd I kame my Hair,
For my true Love has me forsook,
  And says he'll never love me mair.

Now Arthur-Seat shall be my Bed,
  The Sheets shall ne'er be fyl'd by me,   soiled
Saint Anton's Well shall be my Drink,
  Since my true Love has forsaken me.
Martinmas Wind, when wilt thou blaw,
  And shake the green Leaves off the Tree?
O gentle Death, when wilt thou come,
  For of my Life I am weary.

'Tis not the Frost that freezes fell,
  Nor blawing Snaw's Inclemency;

'Tis not sic Cauld that makes my Cry,
  But my Love's Heart grown cauld to me.
When we came in by Glasgow Town,
  We were a comely Sight to see;
My Love was cled in the black Velvet,
  And I my sell in Cramasie.

Crimson

But had I wist before I kis'd,
  That Love had been sae ill to win,
I'd lock'd my Heart in a Case of Gold,
  And pin'd it with a Silver Pin.
Oh oh! if my young Babe were born,
  And set upon the Nurse's Knee,
And I my sell were dead and gane,
  For a Maid again I'll never be.

The Bonny Earl of Murray

Ye Highlands and ye Lawlands,
  Oh! where ha'e ye been:
They ha'e slain the Earl of Murray,
  And they laid him on the Green.

Now wae be to thee, Huntly,
  And wherefore did ye sae;
I bad you bring him wi' you,
  But forbad you him to slae.

He was a braw Gallant,
  And he rid at the Ring;
And the bonny Earl of Murray,
  Oh! he might have been a King.

He was a braw Gallant,
  And he play'd at the Ba',
And the bonny Earl of Murray
  Was the Flower amang them a'.

He was a braw Gallant,
  And he play'd at the Glove,
And the bonny Earl of Murray,
  Oh! he was the Queen's Love.

Oh! lang will his Lady
  Look o'er the Castle-Down,
E'er she see the Earl of Murray,
  Come sounding through the Town.

Willy's Rare and Willy's Fair

'Willy's rare, and Willy's fair,
   And Willy's wond'rous bony;
promised   And Willy heght to marry me,
If   Gin e'er he marry'd ony.

'Yestreen I made my Bed fu' brade,
   The Night I'll make it narrow;
For a' the live-long Winter's Night,
deprived;
Mate   I lie twin'd of my Marrow.

'O came you by yon Water-side,
   Pu'd you the Rose or Lilly;
Or came you by yon Meadow green,
   Or saw you my sweet Willy?'

She sought him East, she sought him West,
   She sought him brade and narrow;
cleft; Crag Sine in the clifting of a Craig,
   She found him drown'd in Yarrow.

Edward, Edward

Why dois your brand sae drap wi' bluid,
    Edward, Edward?
Why dois your brand sae drap wi' bluid?
  And why sae sad gang yee, O?
O, I hae killed my hauke sae guid,
    Mither, mither:
O, I hae killed my hauke sae guid;
  And I had nae mair bot hee, O.

Your haukis bluid was nevir sae reid;
    Edward, Edward.
Your haukis bluid was nevir sae reid;
  My deir son I tell thee, O.
O, I hae killed my reid-roan steid,
    Mither, mither:
O, I hae killed my reid-roan steid,
  That erst was sae fair and frie, O.

Your steid was auld, and ye hae gat mair,
    Edward, Edward:
Your steid was auld, and ye hae gat mair,
  Sum other dule ye drie, O.   grief; bear
O, I hae killed my fadir deir,
    Mither, mither:
O, I hae killed my fadir deir
  Alas! and wae is mee, O!

And whatten penance wul ye drie for that? what kind
    Edward, Edward.   of

And whatten penance will ye drie for that?
    My deir son, now tell me, O.
Ile set my feit in yonder boat,
        Mither, mither:
Ile set my feit in yonder boat,
    And Ile fare ovir the sea, O.

And what wul ye doe wi' your towirs and your ha',
    Edward, Edward?
And what wul ye doe wi' your towirs and your ha',
    That were sae fair to see, O?
Ile let thame stand tul they doun fa',
        Mither, mither:
Ile let thame stand tul they doun fa',
    For here nevir mair maun I bee, O.

And what wul ye leive to your bairns and your wife,
    Edward, Edward?
And what wul ye leive to your bairns and your wife,
    Whan ye gang ovir the sea, O?
The warldis room, late them beg thrae life,
        Mither, mither:
The warldis room, let them beg thrae life,
    For thame nevir mair wul I see, O.

whole world's space; through

And what wul ye leive to your ain mither deir,
    Edward, Edward:
And what wul ye leive to your ain mither deir,
    My deir son, now tell mee, O.
The curse of hell frae me sall ye beir,
        Mither, mither;
The curse of hell frae me sall ye beir,
    Sic counseils ye gave to me, O.

The Lowlands of Holland

'My love has built a bonny ship, and set her on the sea,
With seven score good mariners to bear her company;
There's three score is sunk, and threescore dead at
    sea,
And the lowlands of Holland has twin'd my love   parted
    and me.

'My love he built another ship, and set her on the
    main,
And nane but twenty mariners for to bring her hame,
But the weary wind began to rise, and the sea began
    to rout,   roar
My love then and his bonny ship turn'd withershins   contrary to
    about.   the sun's
                                          course

'There shall neither coif come on my head, nor comb
    come in my hair;
There shall neither coal nor candle light shine in my
    bower mair,
Nor will I love another one, until the day I die,
For I never lov'd a love but one, and he's drown'd in
    the sea.'

'O had your tongue my daughter dear, be still and be
    content,
There are mair lads in Galloway, ye need nae sair
    lament;'
'O! there is nane in Galloway, there's nane at a' for me,
For I never lov'd a love but ane, and he's drown'd in
    the sea.'

The Trumpeter of Fyvie

gates

At Fyvie's yetts there grows a flower,
    It grows baith braid and bonny;
There's a daisie in the midst o' it,

called by
the name
of

    And it's ca'd by Andrew Lammie.

'O gin that flower war in my breast,
    For the love I bear the laddie;
I wad kiss it, and I wad clap it,
    And daut it for Andrew Lammie.

The first time me and my love met,
    Was in the woods of Fyvie;

caress

'He kissed my lips five thousand times,
    And ay he ca'd me bonny;
And a' the answer he gat frae me,
    Was, My bonny Andrew Lammie!'

'Love, I maun gang to Edinburgh;
    Love, I maun gang and leave thee.'
'I sighed right sair, and said nae mair,
    But, O gin I were wi' ye!'

'But true and trusty will I be,
    As I am Andrew Lammie,
I'll never kiss a woman's mouth,
    Till I come back and see thee.'

'And true and trusty will I be,
    As I am Tiftie's Annie;

I'll never kiss a man again,
    Till ye come back and see me.'

Syne he's come back frae Edinburgh,   Then
    To the bonny hows o' Fyvie;   hollows
And ay his face to the nor-east,
    To look for Tiftie's Annie.

'I ha'e a love in Edinburgh,
    Sae ha'e I intill Leith, man;   in
I hae a love intill Montrose,
    Sae ha'e I in Dalkeith, man.

'And east and west where'er I go,
    My love she's always wi' me;
For east and west where'er I go,
    My love she dwells in Fyvie.

'My love possesses a' my heart,
    Nae pen can e'er indite her;
She's ay sae stately as she goes,
    That I see nae mae like her.

'But Tiftie winna gi'e consent
    His dochter me to marry,
Because she has five thousand marks,
    And I have not a penny.

'Love pines away, love dwines away,
    Love, love decays the body;
For love o' thee, oh I must die;
    Adieu, my bonny Annie!'

Her mither raise out o' her bed,
    And ca'd on baith her women:
'What ails ye, Annie, my dochter dear?
    O Annie, was ye dreamin'?

sorrow

'What dule disturb'd my dochter's sleep?
    O tell to me, my Annie!'
She sighed right sair, and said nae mair,
    But, 'O for Andrew Lammie!'

Her father beat her cruellie,
    Sae also did her mother;
Her sisters sair did scoff at her;
    But wae betide her brother!

were not
moderate

Her brother beat her cruellie,
    Till his straiks they werena canny;
He brak her back, and he beat her sides,
    For the sake o' Andrew Lammie.

'O fie, O fie, my brother dear,
    The gentlemen'll shame ye;
The laird o' Fyvie he's gaun by,
    And he'll come in and see me.

ask

'And he'll kiss me, and he'll clap me,
    And he will speer what ails me;
And I will answer him again,
    It's a' for Andrew Lammie.'

Her sisters they stood in the door,
    Sair griev'd her wi' their folly;
'O sister dear, come to the door,
    Your cow is lowin on you.'

'O fie, O fie, my sister dear,
   Grieve me not wi' your folly;
I'd rather hear the trumpet sound,
   Than a' the kye o' Fyvie.   cows

'Love pines away, love dwines away,
   Love, love decays the body;
For love o' thee now I maun die –
   Adieu to Andrew Lammie!'

But Tiftie's wrote a braid letter,   a letter on a
   And sent it into Fyvie,   broad sheet
Saying, his daughter was bewitch'd,
   By bonny Andrew Lammie.

'Now, Tiftie, ye maun gi'e consent,
   And lat the lassie marry.'
'I'll never, never gi'e consent
   To the Trumpeter of Fyvie.'

When Fyvie looked the letter on,
   He was baith sad and sorry:
Says – 'The bonniest lass o' the country-side
   Has died for Andrew Lammie.'

O Andrew's gane to the house-top,
   O' the bonny house o' Fyvie;
He's blawn his horn baith loud and shill   shrill
   O'er the lawland leas o' Fyvie.

'Mony a time ha'e I walk'd a' night,
   And never yet was weary;
But now I may walk wae my lane,   sadly by
   For I'll never see my deary.   myself

'Love pines away, love dwines away,
  Love, love decays the body:
For the love o' thee, now I maun die –
  I come, my bonny Annie!'

Johnnie Faa

The gypsies they came to my Lord Cassillis' yett,   gate
   And O! but they sang bonnie;
They sang sae sweet, and sae complete,
   That down came our fair Ladie.

She came tripping down the stairs,
   And all her maids before her;
As soon as they saw her weel far'd face,   favoured
   They coost their glamourie owre her.   cast; spell

She gave to them the good wheat bread,
   And they gave her the ginger;
But she gave them a far better thing,
   The gold ring off her finger.

'Will ye go with me, my hinny and my heart,   honey
   Will ye go with me, my dearie,
And I will swear, by the staff of my spear,
   That your Lord shall nae mair come near thee?'

'Gar take from me my silk manteel,   Cause
   And bring to me a plaidie,
For I will travel the world owre,
   Along with the Gypsie Laddie.

'I could sail the seas with my Jockie Faa,
   I could sail the seas with my dearie,
I could sail the seas with my Jockie Faa,
   And with pleasure could drown with my dearie.'

They wandred high, they wandred low,
    They wandred late and early,
Untill they came to an old tenant's barn,
    And by this time she was weary.

'Last night I lay in a weel made bed,
    And my noble Lord beside me,
And now I must ly in an old tenant's barn,
scowling   And the black crew glowring owre me.'

'O hold your tongue, my hinny and my heart,
    O hold your tongue, my dearie,
For I will swear by the moon and the stars
    That thy Lord shall nae mair come near thee.'

They wandred high, they wandred low,
    They wandred late and early,
Untill they came to that wan water,
    And by this time she was wearie.

'Aften have I rode that wan water,
    And my Lord Cassillis beside me,
And now I must set in my white feet and wade,
    And carry the Gypsie Laddie.'

By and by came home this noble Lord,
    And asking for his ladie,
The one did cry, the other did reply,
    'She is gone with the Gypsy Laddie.'

'Go saddle to me the black,' he says,
    'The brown rides never so speedie,
And I will neither eat nor drink,
    Till I bring home my Ladie.'

He wandred high, he wandred low,
   He wandred late and early,
Untill he came to that wan water,
   And there he spied his Ladie.

'O wilt thou go home, my hinny and my heart,
   O wilt thou go home, my dearie,
And I'll close thee in a close room
   Where no man shall come near thee?'

'I will not go home, my hinny and my heart,
   I will not go home, my dearie,
If I have brewn good beer I will drink of the same,
   And my Lord shall nae mair come near me.

'But I will swear by the moon and the stars,
   And the sun that shines so clearly,
That I am as free of the gypsie gang
   As the hour my mother did bear me.'

They were fifteen valiant men,
   Black, but very bonny,
And they lost all their lives for one –
   The Earl of Cassillis' Ladie.

Get Up and Bar the Door

It fell about the Martinmas time,
　　And a gay time it was then,
When our goodwife got puddings to make,
　　And she's boil'd them in the pan.

The wind sae cauld blew south and north,
　　And blew into the floor:
Quoth our goodman, to our goodwife,
　　'Gae out and bar the door.'

house-
wifery
'My hand is in my hussy'f skap,
　　Goodman, as ye may see,
An it shou'd nae be barr'd this hundred year,
　　Its no be barr'd for me.'

They made a paction 'tween them twa,
　　They made it firm and sure;
That the first word whae'er shou'd speak,
　　Shou'd rise and bar the door.

Then by there came two gentlemen,
　　At twelve o'clock at night,
And they could neither see house nor hall,
　　Nor coal nor candle light.

'Now, whether is this a rich man's house,
　　Or whether is it a poor?'
But ne'er a word wad ane o' them speak,
　　For barring of the door.

And first they ate the white puddings,
    And then they ate the black;
Tho' muckle thought the goodwife to hersel,
    Yet ne'er a word she spake.

Then said the one unto the other,
    'Here, man, tak ye my knife,
Do ye tak aff the auld man's beard,
    And I'll kiss the goodwife.'

'But there's nae water in the house,
    And what shall we do than?'
'What ails ye at the pudding broo,   water
    That boils into the pan?'

O up then started our goodman,
    An angry man was he;
'Will ye kiss my wife before my een,
    And scad me wi' pudding bree?'

Then up and started our goodwife,
    Gied three skips on the floor;
'Goodman, you've spoken the foremost word,
    Get up and bar the door.'

Index of Titles and First Lines